Grin and Pear it

A Most Unlikely Sequel

D0469652

ADAM BLAIN

About the Author

Adam was born in London in 1970, the youngest of three brothers. After studying law at Cambridge University, Adam spent time working as a teacher in Lesotho, Southern Africa, returning to practise corporate law in London. Following diagnosis of a grade 4 glioblastoma multiforme (GBM) brain tumour in 2014, Adam wrote his first book, *Pear Shaped.* Adam continues to live in London with his wife and three children.

You can follow Adam and his progress on Twitter:
@AdamBBlain

This book is dedicated to those who have lost, or are currently fighting the battle against cancer, as well as to the family, friends and medical staff supporting them.

Contents

Autumn 2016

Introduction

Hello loyal readers. It's me again and guess what? I am not dead yet (at the time of writing this introduction). For those of you who have not read my first book, *Pear Shaped*, let me quickly bring you up to speed. Better still, stop reading now, download Pear Shaped, read it and then come back to this. If you do not have the time, money or inclination to do so, I expect you will pick up the plot pretty quickly. In bullet points:

- Boring middle-class bloke from North London (me!), with a lovely wife (Lu) and three lovely children: Jonah, Sacha (as in the boy's name) and Thea.
- I was diagnosed with a brain tumour, known as grade 4 glioblastoma multiforme or 'GBM'.
- Basically this is Latin for 'Get your affairs in order: you will shortly be dead'. It is also, known affectionately in GBM circles as 'The Terminator'.
- My surgeon performed a huge operation removing a chunk of my brain which was (in his words) the size of a pear.
- The National Health Service (NHS) is superb and employs lovely people.
- I took lots of horrible medicines and underwent revolting treatments including radiotherapy and chemotherapy.
- Terrible survival odds and no sign of a cure on the horizon. On average, the patients diagnosed with this disease survive eighteen months from the date of diagnosis.

- I had survived for 10 months at the end of the first book, so it looked like any sequel was going to have to be an obituary.
- There – I have just saved you £2.99.

As of Autumn 2016, I have somehow managed to avoid a Pear regrowth for thirty months. This means I am now in the top ten percent in terms of survival time which makes me (so far) one of the lucky ones. Only 'lucky' in the sense of a starting point of having GBM. Not lucky like a lottery winner. Pear (or his cousin) could return at any moment, and I never forget this. Indeed, my doctors say that, even after all this time, he WILL come back. The expression you may be looking for is:

BORROWED TIME

Being able to write this sequel is therefore very unexpected and you really should not put money on this 'Pear Series' becoming a trilogy.

Quarterly Scans

After the initial flurry of scans associated with diagnosis and treatment, surviving GBM sufferers get an MRI scan every three months. It is all part of the service. The average person with GBM therefore gets around four of these regular check-up scans (the first six months being taken up with treatment) before terrible news is delivered. I have had eight to date, each one a thumbs up. My next scan is due in a couple of weeks. Things get very tense in the build-up, with several nights of troubled sleep for both Lu and me.

*

After what felt like an eternity, scan day arrived and off we went back to the hospital to see if anything untoward had appeared in my brain over the previous quarter. Except that's not what happened. We may now live in a world where instantaneous satisfaction is just a phone tap away, but my scans need to be checked and double checked before I am given any news. Also, the medics insist that any news (good or bad) is delivered face-to-face.

So, it's back home for another couple of worrying days and troubled nights before returning to the hospital.

*

Waiting to see the oncologist on results day, in the area outside her office, is when my anxiety reaches its peak.

It is my lovely specialist nurse (Hello Eileen!) who comes out to the waiting room to take us in for the results. As she arrives, I search her face for any clue as to the outcome. Like a true pro, Eileen gives nothing away early. I bet she's a fiendish poker player.

In the interests of balance, I would point out that I have never seen Eileen just before a meeting for the delivery of bad news (thank goodness!). Perhaps I just see her normal demeanour, as she actually is. And perhaps, when she knows that bad news is shortly going to be delivered by the consultant, she loses her composure, races into the waiting room rending her uniform and tearing out fistfuls of her own hair whilst wailing up to the heavens:

"IT'S NOT FAIR!!! WHY HIM?!!!"

Then, turning to the patient:

"So, let's pop in to the consultant and get those results."

Naomi, my fabulous oncologist, reveals the results a few seconds later in her office. So far, on each occasion, Lu and I collapse with relief having been told that my scan is 'lovely'. Then Lu and I head off for our 'I'm-Not-Going-to-Die-Imminently' celebratory coffee. What I really needed was a whisky, but the pubs were not open at 10am. I was going to start bringing a hip flask of single malt with me to celebrate but that is making a big assumption, particularly now that fate seems to take such pleasure in kicking me in the balls.

Thinking back, I realise that the news from the scan result is revealed to us by Naomi immediately – even before we sit down. Whilst I am grateful for this humane method of breaking the news, a huge opportunity for fun is being missed here.

The results should be in an envelope which is opened in front of me to the sound of a recorded drum roll. Naomi should then, really slowly, read the results whilst trying to wrong-foot me with mixed messages. A bit like the host of a television game show toying with the contestants. Perhaps even have the results in sealed and over-sized envelopes like they do at the Oscars. The envelopes are opened accompanied by a drum roll. She then says:

"I'm really, really sorry Adam but if you look at the scan you will notice [dramatic pause] if you look at the dark patches on my screen you ...... can cer......cancer [cough] can cer... tainly see the tumour has remained ..... non-visible. You will soon be dead.... [pause] ..... That is: dead chuffed at the result I am about to reveal. Yes, I can see you're definitely about to kick the bucket; I'll move it from by your chair – please hand it back to the cleaner, standing by the door. Without doubt, you will very soon be on your way out....[pause] ....of my office and celebrating. Now let's see what you could have won by looking in the other envelopes. [pause] Oh, that's a shame! You missed out on herpes and rickets. Anyway, you don't go home empty-handed. You take with you brain cancer. Let's have a big hand please for Adam".

New 'Features'

Since developing this horrible disease, I have noticed some changes in me:

- I have a tendency to get ice-cream headaches when I'm in the sunshine.
- My short-term memory is not great.
- In the sunshine, I tend to get ice-cream headaches.
- Now, this is the strangest one: There is a specific point on the top of my head where, if I dig my fingernail in, it makes me sneeze. Clock radios have a snooze button. I have a sneeze button. What's this all about? I cannot claim to have a further superpower in addition to my existing three (you can read *Pear Shaped* for the details of these superpowers). Yet I would also struggle to call it an ailment. It is just a thing – a minor defect in my operating system. Or is it an upgrade that has not yet been rolled out to others? I am not the only one in my family with a sneeze thing. My cousin, Ben, has an on-line video of himself repeatedly making himself sneeze in this way. I have never seen this video because whenever I search under the relevant words, all I get is lots of people sneezing in swimming pools – which I do not want. What is worse is that these are not just *any* people. These are people suffering with diarrhoea and sneezing in a swimming pool. You can guess what happens next; on each occasion the sneezer in question looks like a startled squid and all other swimmers vacate the pool. Who posts this stuff? Who watches this stuff (on purpose)?

Anyway, my team of medics only have a diagnosis for the short-term memory loss. Apparently I'm just a bit thick. At least they have a name for it.

The Little Things

If you think brain cancer puts everything else in perspective, you're wrong. I still have day-to-day hassles like everyone else and it drives me mad. You get the full-blown trauma of a terminal disease as well as the constant background of day-to-day crap that everyone else has. In conversation with anybody at all, I have my Get-Out-of-Jail-Free card of:

"Well at least you haven't got brain cancer."

But this doesn't work on myself, even if adapted to:

"Well at least this is nowhere near as bad as brain cancer."

Instead, I completely lose it when the department store delivers yet another faulty dishwasher. Or the burger chain can't combine the chocolate milkshake ingredients together in the correct proportions. The triviality of having dirty plates piled to the ceiling and paying for a pale beige milkshake is still very annoying – even with cancer. Whilst this disease is a massive pile of crap to deal with, it does not make the smaller things any less irritating. It's just that you have cancer as well!

I also now appreciate that there is no fair portion of misfortune, or that it stops when you have had as much as you can handle. Bad luck can be infinite.

You never reach a stage of having so much misfortune in your life that any more is forbidden by fate or irrelevant to you (and therefore unnoticeable). When I, every morning, bang my head on the corner of the mug cupboard in our kitchen, it hurts just as much, and for just as long, as it would if I were healthy.

Insurance

I am truly grateful that I have survived this long but it is a challenge to remain positive about my future. This is not helped by the fact that my life policy has just paid out. They did this quite unperturbed by the fact that I am in correspondence with them, and not even under a pseudonym. This is no elaborate fraud. I have been totally open with the insurer about my 'alive' status. I can only rationalise two possible reasons for their behaviour:

1) The insurance company is thinking:
   Let's not split hairs here. You have effectively left the party (of the living). You're just collecting your coat from the cloakroom. Don't forget that little ticket!
2) This could be like the film *The Sixth Sense* [spoiler alert if you haven't seen it]. Perhaps I am dead but just do not know it. After all, there is no way an insurance company would pay out otherwise. Also, with my brain damage, I often make mistakes and insurance companies tend not to – particularly when paying out. So, as with most things that confuse me, I check with Lu who is very frank with me on all medical matters. She assures me that I am not dead and is quite convincing in putting forward this contention. So un-dead, in fact, that I kicked her quite hard in my sleep last night.

So it turns out, my policy pays out on critical illness. There are certainly perks to this whole dying malarkey.

Going to the GP

I do not go the doctor very often. I mean my General Practitioner (GP), not my hospital doctors. The latter I see quarterly and, without exception, they are lovely and helpful. However, I have developed an aversion to seeking medical help if I don't think it is serious. Some might say this is due to being diagnosed with a terminal illness, undergoing debilitating treatment and having to visit hospital on a regular basis to receive potentially life-threatening news. They would be right.

So I find myself downplaying anything that happens to me in terms of illness or injury. Inevitably though, if the ailment worsens or fails to disappear on its own, Lu convinces me that I require the uplifting experience of a visit to the GP surgery.

Do you:

- Hate your job and would hate any job?
- Have terrible people skills?
- Have a truly awful telephone manner?
- Love the word 'No', particularly when used in the phrase 'No, you can't'?
- Generally have a negative and difficult personality?
- Find that people gravitate away from you at parties, leaving a social vacuum around you wherever you drift?

Then you should consider a job as a receptionist for a GP surgery. Do not merely pretend to have these attributes – you really must be a negative, rude and difficult person. Apparently people like this do not always have to work for the local council.

To be a GP receptionist, you must be able to say 'No' to all of the following questions, when asked by a patient:

- Can you please post to me my medical report, this time without me having to send to you a stamped, self-addressed envelope (SAE)?
- I sent you an SAE, which you acknowledged that the surgery had both received and then subsequently lost. Now can you post me that report?
- So, here I am. I have taken time off work and I have come back in with a stamp, a pen and remembering my name and address. By the way, could I please have an envelope?
- You apparently don't have envelopes, but there is that huge stationery cupboard right behind you, in which I can see a giant box three-quarters full of unused envelopes. So can I create my own SAE (as the report is not yet ready to collect) given that I am providing the expensive bit i.e. the stamp?
- Can I make an appointment to see one of the doctors?
- No appointments available? I see. So how about the next available appointment, whenever that may be? I am only suffering a little bit with terminal brain cancer, so the appointment can be far into the future. No problem waiting; I have up to eighteen months left to live. So can I please have the next free slot whenever that is, assuming it is within the next eighteen months?

- My wife is also a patient here. If I die before the date of this proposed, cherished appointment, can I bequeath my appointment to her in my Will?
- You inform me that the books are 'not yet open' for any future appointments. I cannot pitch up at 8.30 in the morning (as you suggest) on the off-chance an appointment becomes available. I have to take my daughter to school at that time. So how about you make an exception to this very sensible rule, bearing in mind that I'm a little bit dying of cancer?
- You know the appointments that are 'not yet open'? Please can you open one?

If the word 'Yes' appears in any answer, then you are not qualified to be a GP receptionist.

Having failed to make an appointment, I explain over the phone that I need to see a doctor. This is where the fun starts:

Receptionist: *"Is it urgent?"*

Me: *"I don't think so, but I don't know. I'm not a doctor."*

Receptionist: *"What is the problem?"*

Me: *"So you are medically qualified?"*

Receptionist: *"No"*

Me: *"But you can diagnose or triage me, and can do so over the phone?"*

Receptionist: *"Mr Blain, I'm trying to help you. What seems to be the problem?"*

Me: *"I have this excessive discharge from my left ear, right nostril and both eyes."*

Receptionist: *"What is the discharge like?"*

Me: *"It's blue"*

(I don't really have this disease, but I am dead curious as to what illness has these symptoms and what the receptionist's diagnosis will be.)

Me: *"Also, I have just developed this ringing sound."*

Receptionist: *"In your ears?"*

Me: *"No, in my left leg."* [face palm myself]

Me (continuing): *"Don't worry about that – forget it. It was the doorbell. Just someone at the door delivering a parcel. Let's go back to your understanding of blue-goo disease."*

This is another reason I do not see the GP often – because I cannot get past the receptionist. If I were to persevere, by the time I manage to get an appointment, my ailment will have either killed me, hospitalised me or will have resolved itself. None of which require the input of a GP.

Being a Lawyer

I love being a corporate lawyer. It is like having a job solving puzzles and arguing with people (two of my favourite pastimes). It's a challenging job that uses intellect for every aspect. Putting together and closing a deal is satisfying and gives me a sense of worth. There is also the benefit of having an income. However, the challenge and self-respect of being a lawyer are most important to me. Money is secondary. Really!

I was a corporate lawyer when Pear first revealed himself. The NHS did what they could to get rid of Pear and then get me on my feet, as I have outlined in *Pear Shaped*.

After my initial treatment, I assumed I was meant to lie in bed and wait to die. Yet I didn't feel like doing that. Nor did I want to mope around the house feeling sorry for myself. So I went back to work a mere five months after surgery.

I pre-warned them, of course. I did not just pitch up one day in my hospital gown, head bandaged and staggering around like an extra from *Night of the Living Dead*. However, I didn't want any fancy greetings or re-introductions. Just back to my screen and desk as if nothing had happened.

It did not go quite like that.

The first commute on my return to work was terrifying. Was the tube always this crowded and aggressive? But I managed a successful journey without any major problems, despite Pear getting most of my navigation skills.

However, I knew things had changed when I walked in to the office.

Firstly, people were understandably different with me. Some were very concerned and sympathetic. Others looked a little baffled to see me there, as I staggered around bald, scarred and a little dazed.

Secondly, I could not find my desk. What floor did I work on? This was embarrassing. I quickly checked the phone list on display and realised my work home was on floor two. I remembered being next to a window. Having located my desk, I then found the most important item – the coffee pot – and got back to my files.

Being a corporate lawyer is a tough job at the best of times and I was beginning to realise that the job was virtually impossible without a right temporal lobe. In other words, along with navigation, the 'law skills' bit of my brain clearly resided in Pear. A loss to the legal profession, perhaps, unless some firm wants to take Pear out of the hospital freezer and defrost him, before wiring him in to a PC and the latest online dictaphone technology.

After several months of trying to be the person I had been, it all became too much. At the ripe old age of forty-six, I retired on the basis of ill health. Technically, I decided to retire, although it was not really a 'decision'. It was a 'decision' in the same way an eighteen-stone hod carrier might 'decide' never to be an Olympic gymnast. With cancer, it's not just your health you lose.

*

As one door closes, another opens and my new career of house-husband and child carer is underway (a 'Manny' as they are called round these parts if you are looking after somebody else's kids.). Questions like:

"How do I structure and negotiate this ten-million-pound investment to the best possible benefit of my client?"
have become:

"How do I sort this washing so that all the whites are together and yet there is still plenty of space on the drying rack for when the coloureds and woollens have finished their cycles?"

Alternative Meds

As additional treatment for this disease, I am taking various supposed alternative remedies (as well as the doctor-approved ones).

There are so many things out there being put forward as a 'cure'. I've yet to find something that nobody thinks is a cure, or at least has beneficial properties for someone in my position.

Most 'cures' are found on the internet. It still drives me mad deciding what to participate in. The medics say: "*It's all rubbish.*" The non-medics say: "*What do the medics know?*"

In terms of what to eat or drink, no two people agree on anything. We cancer sufferers are pretty vulnerable because of the constant worry that a cure is right under our nose, yet ignored.

I maintain a compromise position and only take supplements or alternative remedies if they satisfy all of the following criteria:

1) There is some support from the medical/scientific community. Or at least it does not make an oncologist burst out laughing. Doctor This or Professor That must somewhere put their name to this substance.

2) The cure does not come to me in any unsolicited manner. This rules out anything that finds me from the internet.

3) It is not massively expensive. Not because money would necessarily be my obstacle to this 'cure' – it just makes it smell scam-like. So, irrespective of the economics behind it, a requested payment up front of $250 for a vial of special

water to be shipped to me from the United States just has to be a con and stinks of scam. Something in the two-for-one bucket at the local health food shop smells like a freshly cut English lawn by comparison.

4) The 'cure' is generally available so whoever is pushing it cannot earn enough money to make it worthwhile as a scam. I think it extremely unlikely that I am inadvertently buying fake turmeric; or that my garlic is being cut with extract of lesser vegetables.
5) It is nothing very dangerous or unpleasant to take (although see garlic issues below and comments on apricot kernels).

I note that there are many therapies for cancer on offer involving coffee enemas, which seem mainly to be located in Mexico. Yes, you read that correctly. It was not autocorrect on my laptop. Coffee enemas. I have so many questions regarding this treatment:

i) The very first question (and most obvious) has to be: How the hell did they discover it 'worked'? Must have been a very quiet afternoon in the lab, possibly just before the Christmas party kicked off. Also, what had they previously tried on this route to finding the 'cure'? Were all trials based upon the use of beverages? Or were they working through an alphabetically ordered list of all substances to see what had the best results. First attempt was aardvark extract. The penultimate round of experiments (prior to discovering the wonders of coffee) was based upon cob-nuts.

ii) Do they cool the coffee down before squirting it in? Alternatively, in the summer, can you get an 'Enema-frappuccino' to cool you down and is it as calorific as the oral version?

iii) Finally, each time you attend the clinic for this treatment, do you get your little loyalty card stamped so that the tenth enema is free?

Which prompts me to mention a further criterion for a supposedly curative substance, namely that the point of entry of a substance must be above my midriff. Surprisingly, I have elected to have nothing squirted up my back side.

Applying these rules, I am currently taking:

- Green tea.
- Turmeric extract.
- Apricot kernels.
- Garlic capsules.

These herbals at least make me feel like I'm doing something. So I take these twice a day (or when I have a cup of tea in respect of the green tea) but it's not all plain sailing. Nothing is quite as unpleasant as a full on, lingering, garlic burp whilst half way through one's breakfast granola.

You may think that the use of these rules is a rather random way to find a 'cure' but at least I feel I am doing something, which is important to me. The trouble is, if I do stumble across the magical treatment and live to the ripe old age of, say, fifty, nobody will be able to tell which of the cocktail of supplements was the one that worked. So, I will be no use whatsoever to the researchers.

Let me dwell on one of my hope giving supplements: apricot kernels. This must have been one of the greatest pieces of marketing ever. An apricot kernel is a small nut that resides in the centre of an apricot stone. A lot of people do not know that there is a nut in there. Why would they bother to check? This nut tastes bitter and has very high levels of cyanide. So, some very bright spark has taken the waste product from another process (the production of apricot jam or tinned apricots), which tastes disgusting and is poisonous, and sold it on. As the product could be sourced for no cost, the mark-up must be huge (or infinite, on a percentage basis). Don't forget, they only have to go round the back of the jam factory, look in the bins and take what they want. This bitter, toxic, freely available waste product is then sold to the gullible at £10 a throw. Which is where I come in to the picture. I have been taking them for a year and, at the time of writing, I am not dead. In terms of internet chat room rules, there's your proof. As they are fairly poisonous given their cyanide content, I believe these kernels could be legitimately marketed with a slogan such as:
"Eat enough of these and we guarantee you won't die of cancer."

Weight Loss

Have you ever had one of those dreams where you are in public and then suddenly realise you are naked? Well, I was not dreaming.

There I was taking my morning constitutional walk when my trousers fell down. Not all the way to the pavement – that would be ridiculous. But below my buttocks. Too much to be a trendy, youngster fashion statement. More like a toddler learning to dress themselves whilst wearing a full nappy. I was forced to hold my trousers up, and waddle back home to drill a new hole in my belt.

You see, a side effect of one of my many medications is that I have no appetite. Since the operation, I have lost about 15% of my body mass. My Body Mass Index (BMI) category has changed from:

"Bit chubby, if you ask me"

into [Jewish-mother voice]:

"Eat something, for God's sake!"

I am in the enviable position where I need to gain weight. Or is it enviable? For me, eating was a great pleasure – particularly the sensation of satisfying hunger with decent grub. But I do not get hungry. Instead, a kind of empty nausea descends, and with it, a feeling of repulsion towards anything edible.

*

Yesterday, I went to see the doctor about my rapid depletion. Whilst he did not prescribe chocolate, he did recommend it.

Specifically, Cadbury's Whole Nut as it has nuts as well as chocolate (obviously – clue is in the name). That is about the best thing your GP can possibly say to you. Right at the opposite extreme of the spectrum from:

"Please lie down on the couch so I can conduct this prostate examination. I must warn you, I have very large, cold hands."

The principles behind weight gain are simple – take all the concepts from dieting and simply reverse them. Books on how to gain weight (aside from body-building ones) are pretty hard to come by. However, there are loads of dieting books. To create your own weight gain book, simply buy a dieting book and a pen. Change every reference of 'do' to 'don't' and references of 'never' to 'go on – do it'. Change every method of cooking specified to 'frying'. So,

"Gently steam that kale"

becomes

"Make sure you deep fry it in batter. And don't start with kale – use cheese."

Likewise,

"Low fat hummus eaten off celery sticks is a tasty treat."

becomes

"Make sure you choose the fattiest hummus (you know, the one with a pool of oil on the top) and buy a bucket of it. Instead of using carrot sticks or other crudités, try dunking Cadbury's Flakes or KitKat fingers."

So, you want a snack to get you through to supper time? Forget fruit. Have a quick dessertspoon of butter, sweetened with some syrup. Brighten this snack up with some coloured, sugar sprinkles.

I have discovered snacks that would cause dieters to quake in their boots. Peanuts are not calorific enough. There is protein, fibre and other such rubbish getting in the way of my salty, fatty goodness. There is also an absence of refined carbohydrate, like sugar.

Whilst browsing the snack aisle of my local supermarket, I found a solution. Peanuts that are covered in caramel, dipped in sesame seeds and then fried. As they are both sweet and savoury, you can eat them as nibbles before, during and after any meal. The only issue is the nine or ten calories expended trying to get the packet open.

How to Eat a Meal with my Brothers

As just mentioned, eating has become a stressful chore. Let me give you a scenario where this becomes an outright challenge.

I have two older brothers: Martin and Nick. Growing up with them means I have had thousands of meals in their company. Whilst many parts of our fraternal relationship have matured and become more civilised, eating with them has not evolved into something that could be classified as 'grown up'. Without parents to adjudicate, this has actually regressed.

The aim of a meal with my brothers, obviously, is to get the most food. Inevitably this will be at the expense of the other siblings. See references below to Natural Selection.

For the purposes of explanation, I will pick a brothers' curry at a local Indian restaurant where all food has been pre-agreed as communal. However, the same principles apply anywhere you eat with siblings and there is some communal component to the allotment of food, hence competition for it. For this reason, I exclude buffets or any other scenario where the food source is considered effectively infinite (i.e. more than we can individually or collectively eat). I am also excluding times when there is 'enough' food delivered to your table, as I see no point in dealing with a scenario which is entirely theoretical.

Back to my brothers' curry. Here are the principles of participation and tactics to be adopted if you wish to avoid starvation. Here we go (in no particular order):

Principle 1

Usually there will be communal food and food that it is (or

becomes) yours. 'Yours' can mean ordered specifically and solely for you, or food that has made it to your plate.

Principle 2

Once food has made it to your plate, it is 'yours' and can be eaten at leisure.

Principle 3

Whilst you (obviously) do not need to be polite, you (at least) have to give a nod to eating etiquette. You have to *pretend* you are being polite. Let me give you an example – the waiter, totally oblivious to the scheming going on, stupidly delivers four samosas to the three of us. The guy is obviously either an idiot or is doing this to be provocative – perhaps as some kind of social experiment. Grabbing and scoffing the last samosa (when you have had one each) is rude and so off limits. However, this can be remedied by throwing in a casual comment of pseudo concern:

"You've both had a samosa, haven't you?"

or

"Anyone mind if I...."

Then we get into mind games and psychology, the details of which are beyond the scope of this book but can be obtained from attending one of my lectures on this subject, which tour nationally.

Tactic 1

I am not exactly sure if this counts as a principle or a tactic – it could be argued both ways. I will leave the categorisation for you to decide: A plate is not merely a 'work space' for food or a device to keep your food off the table. It is your reservoir.

Tactic 2

Order a dish that nobody else likes. This does not work with my brothers as they eat absolutely anything – like two farmyard goats sticking their heads out between barbed wire. See Tactic 3 regarding when to eat it.

Tactic 3

Order of eating. Obviously eat communal food first and 'your' food last. Of the communal food, attack it in order of popularity, leaving any unpopular dishes until last. In the unlikely event you manage to order a dish that only you like, basic common sense dictates this is eaten last, together with your reservoir food (see below).

Tactic 4

Fill your plate and fill it high, as if your life depended upon it, even if it means all the different curries blend into one generic curry-rice-naan goo. They are still calories and you are only accelerating the blending process by a few minutes – this will happen inside your stomach anyway.

Tactic 5

Whenever the opportunity arises, eat directly from the central, communal food. So, you could casually dip your naan bread in a central curry or nab a piece of chicken tikka in passing, accompanied with a comment such as

"Oh, didn't see that there. Let me just taste this one."

or

"That looks like it's just about to fall on to the table."

However, limits are required to comply with social etiquette. Naan dipping is allowed (as mentioned). Mixing rice into a central pot for you alone is bad form indeed – you cannot extend your plate territory into centralised crockery.

Tactic 6

Time to start eating off your plate. However, under no circumstances should you eat everything on it. To clear your plate now is akin to a country eating all food reserves shortly before the known arrival of a famine. Eat approximately a fifth of what is on your (hopefully) groaning plate. Eat a bit and replenish, eat and replenish. This way, if the unthinkable occurs and central reserves are emptied prematurely, you have at least eighty percent of your plateful to fall back on. Replenish using Tactic 4.

You are now at the point where all central reserves have been depleted. It is time to start eating all you have left. The stressful part of the evening is over, and you can eat your plateful at leisure. Famine is here so time to plunder the reservoir. There are also the opportunities for trading and deals to be struck.

Having applied my Principles, I will assume that you have suitable quantities of desirable curries to give you the upper hand in these trade negotiations. There is no point me giving the exchange rates. At the time of writing, one onion bhaji was equivalent to 23% of a main course curry. However, exchange rates constantly vary depending upon supply and demand. Those over-investing in one dish, for legal reasons, must be warned that exchange rates can go down as well as up. My advice is to spread your curry portfolio.

With these simple Principles and Tactics, you are guaranteed to leave a meal with my brothers both full and mentally shattered.

More Side Effects

There are various drugs I am taking to ward off Pear's return. My least favourite is called Metformin. It is meant for diabetics (which I am not) and comes with a side effect – terrible diarrhoea. This hits me for some reason at 1.00pm sharp. How do they do that? It would be like a new skin treatment which warns:

"This product may cause skin irritation at 2.45pm."

My whole life went in to a tail spin last week. Diarrhoea came when I least expected it – at noon of all times. It was 11.30am. My contractions had already started and were getting closer and closer together. I had to sprint to the lavatory before I became fully dilated. What was going on? I must have got a duff batch of pills from the pharmacy. Then the penny dropped – the clocks had gone back the previous night. Can they not allow for this in the chemical formula? Millions of people will have their routines completely thrown out twice a year.

Living with such side effects and the negative impact they have on my now reduced life got me thinking. Everything would be so much simpler and convenient without this disease. Let us suppose, whilst clearing out the loft, I discover an old, dusty lamp. You know the routine from here: I polish it up and a genie appears; he grants me a single wish. He is a bit less generous than the traditional genie, so I do not get the second or third wish. He also insists that I use the wish purely for my own selfish purposes. No global peace, saving the planet or other such frivolities. It has got to be for me. So, I can focus on my own issues and use it, say, to rid myself of my belly button fluff plague once and for all. However impressive and extensive this fluff problem may be, it probably is not worth my one and only wish. After all, I do kind of love those little fluff balls I give birth to and the extraction is quite fun.

So, would I use this wish to rid myself of cancer? Of course I bloody would! However, there may be a hesitation before making the choice. Not because something else is vying for that wish. It is just that, in some ways, I am a little bit attached to the disease. Yes – absolutely bizarre! I have spent the last three years trying to clear myself of cancer and yet I would hesitate before actually doing so. Brain cancer is my thing – the thing that makes me unique to my friends, family, colleagues and others who know me. It gives me disabled parking and free tube travel. It also gives me a get-out-of-jail-free-card to win any argument and generally makes me special and worthy of sympathy.

I seem to have developed a version of Stockholm Syndrome with cancer being the evil kidnapper. This disease is complicated in every way.

Things that Keep Me Awake at Night

I am struggling to sleep at the moment. Strangely, my worries are not about cancer, death or dying. That should be what really disturbs me, but I seem to have run out of worry for these subjects. The tanks are empty. I need to let my worry out on other things. Luckily, I have plenty of other stuff that goes round and round my head, stopping me getting a nice slumber. Random things such as:

1) How can one tell when rice cakes have gone stale?
2) Is it 'herds of elephant' or 'herds of elephant*s*'?
3) Why has our cleaner started washing the blankets that sit on top of our bed-sheets every week?

I do not know the Albanian phrase for:
"Stop washing our blankets!"

As a rule of thumb, I wash the blankets in our house once every...never. I never wash my blankets. Does that make me disgusting? Blankets do not touch you often, at least not your skin. Admittedly, they can get a little grubby. They are also a bit scratchy, but this is where the miracle of cotton sheets comes in – to protect you from scratchy, germy hell. However anally retentive you are about cleanliness, I do not recommend washing your blankets once a week. As well as being unnecessary, I can tell you from bitter experience that blankets take a week to dry. So, washing all our blankets each week is, effectively, the same as taking all our blankets away and burning them. Probably worse for the environment too.

Winter 2016

Fame

Today was surprising. I was walking to the shops to buy (amongst other things) some supposedly fresh rice cakes and a kilo of garlic capsules when suddenly I was stopped by a teenager who said:

"Are you that author who wrote a book about brain cancer? It's sick."

For readers who are unfamiliar with 'yoof-speak', 'sick' is a good thing like 'cool'. It is an adjective. I do not think the translation works for 'sick' as a noun (i.e. what you see on the pavement outside pubs on a Saturday morning). You also have to be very careful how you use this expression with grown-ups. For example, you can't go round to someone's house for dinner and when asked if you like the lamb casserole, respond:

"Yeh, it's totally like – sick."

The hosts will then be worried that they put too much carrot in it.

I am quite easy to recognise as I am going bald. However, my hair is not receding in the traditional sense of the baldness emanating from my crown. Instead, 'ground zero' is my right temple – a side effect from radiotherapy. It is quite distinctive, although not in a good sense.

Anyway, I wanted to sound young and cool to this teenager, so I replied, in what I persuaded myself is my natural way of speaking:

"Yo innit bro. Them other books is mingin'. I just strollin' to Budgens to pick my sorry ass up some organic hummus, rice cakes and low-salt roasted cashews."

*

So, it appears I have become a little bit famous. I stress 'little bit'. Certainly not an 'A' lister or even a 'B' lister. However, I believe I am definitely on the correct side of 'K'. Therefore, if you lined up everyone in the country in order of famousness (with the Queen at one end and just some random bloke at the other), I would be in the top fifty percent. My fame does not sound so impressive put in these terms, so I shall call myself an 'F-list celebrity'. Probably at the same level as the person who used to do the singing on the *Shake n' Vac* adverts, or maybe one of the retired Milky Bar Kids who is now old, wrinkly and has lost their cute blonde hair (or retained it, but it now comes out of their ears). So not a complete nobody, but hardly (yet) a household name.

To help reach my fan(s), I set up a Twitter account, though I quickly realised I had very little to say in 140 characters. I tend to waffle – which you will have realised having got this far. However, our very lovely friend Josie came to the rescue and offered to manage the account for me. She has a good insight into what my life is like and therefore could send the occasional tweet for me.

In her role as 'Adam', Josie was quick to respond to news or communications. She was upbeat and positive, as well as not forgetting the log in details and password. In the end I just left tweeting to her as she was better at it than I was, always saying the right kind of things. In her role as 'Adam', she is more effective than I am. So, I am inadequate even at carrying out the role of being myself.

*

Another reason I am recognisable is that there have been several national newspaper articles about my illness and subsequent need to go on about it in print (my first book, *Pear Shaped*, is still available at all good stockists). As part of this, we have had press photographers come to the house to take snaps of myself and the family.

Each time, we are told what to wear. No prominent brand names but, otherwise, wear whatever you are comfortable in – what I would normally wear at the weekend. Likewise, we are asked to relax and appear totally natural.

So, I present myself at the makeshift studio set up in our kitchen wearing only slippers and boxer shorts. I enter the room scratching and adjusting. Apparently when they say 'natural' and 'comfortable' there are limitations.

Another Scan

It's time to visit hospital again for a game of:

'Am I Going to Die this Quarter?'

I know that any day now, I could wake up buried. Or in an urn on the mantelpiece, next to those nice photos of the kids. I feel bad because my ongoing survival seems like it is at the expense of other GBM sufferers. So I am racked with guilt, but still have the anxiety that my time will come. That is certain (and I don't mean when I am seventy).

Receiving my scan results brings this all sharply into focus. I am granted a further three months' of life which means I am now in the top few percent of survivors. I am one of the best performing terminally ill people with brain cancer:

"Yippee – let's get the bunting out!"

Childhood Pets

As a boy, I kept various rodents as pets. It was not feasible to have a dog and nobody in my family is a particular fans of cats. So before I progressed to the *ultimate* rodent pet (which I will get to later) there were a couple of small mammals that joined our family. A hamster called Max and a gerbil named Wilf. These animals were quite fun, particularly Max who had a sense of adventure as well as quite a dark sense of humour.

Max was a genuine part of the family, often sitting down with us at meal times. Strangely, Max was permitted to sit on the table and eat his meal with us. One morning, I was having breakfast with my brother Martin and, of course, Max. Martin was eating a bowl of muesli, as was Max – the same bowl. Martin was quite happy for Max to reach in and grab the odd nut or flake. After all, it was a big bowl of cereal and hamsters do not eat much. In the course of this food sharing, a particularly juicy sultana was spotted by Max right in the centre of the bowl and out of his reach. Fortunately for Max, a spoon was balanced across the rim and the bowl left unattended. This was an opportunity for Max to try out his tightrope walking skills. I suppose I could have stopped him, but where is the fun in that? I had to know if he would succeed. So I allowed Max to walk carefully across the precarious spoon using his best balancing skills. He did well, reaching the centre without any mishap. However, it was here, above the sultana in question, that disaster/hilarity struck depending upon your perspective. If you were Martin – disaster. If you were Max/me – hilarity.

As he reached over to grab the sultana, the spoon flipped over and dumped Max upside down in the centre of the bowl. Now came the gross bit. Martin casually fished him out, brushed off chunks of muesli and wrung out as much milk as possible from Max's fur back into the bowl. Then Martin finished off the bowl of cereal undeterred by hamster dandruff, germs and the like.

As an adult, I am now well beyond hamsters and gerbils, but I do enjoy animal company. In my situation, you need patience and affection – more than can be provided by humans. You need a special pet. I would love a dog but it simply isn't practical at present. I'm not really a cat person: those condescending looks and the certain knowledge that it would kill me if I were much smaller. Looks like I will have to struggle on with human kindness alone.

Of Cats & Rats

Despite not being their biggest fan, I do have experience of living with cats. When I first met Lu, she came with a cat. It was part of the package. So when we moved in together Lentil, her cat, joined our household. To be clear, I did not pick the name Lentil. Lu did this pre-me, hence before I could apply some common sense to the situation. The name was a nod to Lu's vegetarianism. It was picked because 'Soya-Based Mince' is not a nice name nor, for that matter, a nice food.

Although I am not mad on cats, Lentil was a sweet little rescue tortoiseshell. As timid as anything – scared of her own shadow. She did not do the usual cat thing of bringing in dead rodents, frogs and birds. These were much too fearsome as opponents for her – even with these enemies in a state of death. In fact, when we had a mouse infestation (mouse singular, because we were infested by a single mouse), I had to deal with it. It was Lentil's big moment and she blew it. She hid under the sofa whilst I went round on hands and knees chasing the mouse. The expression: *'Just one job to do'* springs to mind. As does the rhetorical question: *'Why buy a dog and bark yourself?'*

It was not as if Lentil took over some of my chores and started watering and fertilising the garden. OK, bad example. It was not as if Lentil started putting the bins out.

So Lentil was a big softy (although not particularly big) and her greatest challenge happened in Lu's old flat. A big prize fight with, in the Red Corner, Lentil the cat and in the Blue

Corner, a moth (to my knowledge, unnamed). Despite her timidity, Lentil was the clear favourite. After all, how could she possibly lose given the size difference and the moth's total lack of weaponry?

Over the course of an entire weekend, the moth and Lentil drove each other mad. Lentil took continuous swipes at the moth with her claws, but each time missed due to some pretty acrobatic flying manoeuvres. In retaliation, the moth was infuriating the cat by constantly dive-bombing her and swerving away at the last second. Dive-bomb, then swipe; over and over again. A total stalemate that the moth seemed to enjoy as the tormentor.

In the end, Lentil got lucky and one of her swipes found its target. The moth came down like a damaged spitfire with its engine on fire. The elated Lentil celebrated by eating the stricken moth.

A victory for Lentil you would assume? No. Lentil then spent the next two days vomiting up moth parts and looking very sorry for herself. So it ended (by my assessment) as a nil-nil draw. The true loser was Lu, who had to clean up all the partially digested moth pieces from various areas of carpet.

Despite such hiccups, I think the good of owning a pet far outweighs the bad. Having ruled out felines and canines, inspiration struck and I have become a rat owner. Not just one – multiple. Yes, I'm serious. They are lovely, affectionate, sociable creatures. They also have the added advantage that we can't really get another cat now, can we?

Here are the answers to the questions I inevitably get asked about these pets:

- No, they don't carry plague.
- No, they don't live in the sewers. They're a PET i.e. an animal that has been selected to live in my home. So, if they live in sewers, so do I; and I don't.
- They eat largely what we do, not human flesh. You think we eat that? Anyway, Lu is vegetarian.
- They are extremely clean, washing themselves and each other constantly, much like a cat (although cats are too selfish to groom other cats).
- No, I don't wash them myself – I find their fur sticks to my tongue.

These responses do not convince everyone. In many cases, my outburst of pro-rat public relations is met with a blank stare. My words might just as well have been as follows:

"You know what I keep as pets? Bit unusual but they are the most rewarding companions, dead easy and cheap to keep. I have a dozen or so wasps. They really are the loveliest pests – I mean pets. We feed them on jam with the odd patch of dried-up beer for a treat."

"You know that fuzzy bit on their head section? Guess what happens if you stroke a wasp gently on that part? It has to be gentle and you must stroke in the direction that the fuzz is growing. Try it and you'll see... Of course it will sting you. They hate it. I was just trying to warn you."

"We lost Jerome last week, which was sad for everybody – particularly the kids. But they have to learn some time about life and death. Please stand and raise a glass with us to our beloved Jerome 'Stingy' Blain. It was a moving ceremony after which he was left to dehydrate slowly in the double glazing and turn into a shell. Jerome – he was such a character! Remember that time Sacha was drinking a glass of coke and Jerome was balancing on one of the ice cubes like a surfer. He was hilarious (Jerome that is, not Sacha). We will bury him with the detached antenna, bitten off by his friend (Montgomery) when their play-fighting got out of hand. Those boys – always up to mischief!"

So Poppy and Coco came to live with us. We got them to help me cope with not working; for me to have a new project and company during the day. Oh yes – and for the kids. To be clear, we are back to rats now and this next bit has nothing to do with wasps.

When Lu and I go out for sushi I inevitably retain our disposable chopsticks and then give them to the rats to gnaw on. This helps keep their teeth in good order. Once, I left a set of chopsticks on their food dish which caused my then six-year -old daughter, Thea, no end of confusion:

"How do they manage to use them? They don't have hands."

The truth was too mundane so I explained that they had not yet worked them out, but they'd get there. Obviously, it comes more naturally to rats originating from Eastern Asia.

Date Night

Lu and I made a mutual commitment a few years ago and we've stuck to it: Thursday is Date Night. Nothing flash, just an hour or two at a local eatery to catch up and be in each other's company. Occasionally work stuff may have to take priority. Other than that, Date Night is sacrosanct.

Tonight, we ended up at our local Thai eatery, even though I have a problem with Thai restaurants. Not the food – I love Thai food. It's the beautiful Thai waitress who opens the door and welcomes you. The greeting is a graceful bow and herein lies the problem. When the Thai waitress bows to you, how do you respond? You don't want to get it wrong. I make a point to never to offend anybody who may be handling my food in the near future. Here are my possible responses to the bow from the waitress together with their associated problems:

1) A gracious wave coupled with a slightly bemused expression *à la* Prince Philip being forced to watch a native dance on one of his tours. Bit patronising.
2) Bow back. Hang on – no! Not my culture and I may be doing it wrong in a way that's insulting and therefore inadvertently racist. There is also the not insignificant risk of a clash of heads as we both descend simultaneously. In any culture, it cannot be polite to head-butt someone in the face. What if a bow is not a thing to respond to in Thai society? Imagine going to a distant land and every time you blow your nose, those nearby face you respectfully and blow their noses in response.

3) Respond with a greeting of one's own culture. So if you're Italian – a kiss on each cheek. Eskimos – rub noses. For me it's a Jewish shrug and a very British awkward half smile, together with (and this is the clever bit) a very slight inclination of the head. This ambiguously represents a return bow or a nod of greeting and/or approval. Perfect. Far too vague to cause offence.

Then we are seated and presented with an unwanted bowl of prawn crackers which are crunchy, oily and salty yet actually contain no nutrition. Aahhh – prawn crackers – the Thai 'popadom'. They are completed with a little bowl of goo that's radioactive orange in colour and bound to give you cancer.

Whenever we go out as a couple (Lu and I, that is, not the waitress), we spend the first half hour synchronising diaries. This is the bit I hate as it brings home how forgetful I have become and how bad I am at maintaining a diary.

When we dine with other couples, there are topics that I am not allowed to talk about e.g. mathematics (which I have taught in the past). Apparently, I am a bit of a bore and talk far too much about this subject. I have this speciality where I describe a fictional scenario at an egg farm. By the end, our bored companions can count and do basic arithmetic in base six. I am now absolutely banned from doing this ever again. It is most unfair. I cannot talk about my favourite topic, yet Lu has no restrictions on talking about the kids.

*

We sometimes eat in a local pub. Steak & chips with a pint of ale and I am in heaven. However, one thing has started to bother me about pub food. Why are menus becoming so full of 'pulled' dishes? I would like to have my say about 'pulled' meat; you know, pulled chicken and the like. From absolutely nowhere, it is now all the rage. However, for me, as well as not liking pulled chicken I also hate the name and find it very off-putting. 'Pulled' is a terrible expression to use when describing a method of removing meat from bone. 'Pulled' is an expression which, when meaning 'extraction', should be reserved only for bogies. Furthermore, the expression is spoiling other expressions. After a gym session, a pulled hamstring now sounds like a sandwich filler.

In terms of words to describe meat extracted from a carcass in an appetising way, 'pulled' is one of the worst expressions that can be used. It is exceeded in horribleness only by the verbs:

'picked', 'coiled', 'rubbed', 'oozed' and 'crimped off'.

Whilst mentioning pubs, I would also like to recount a meal I had with my brother-in-law and his household. We went to a pub called *The Bull* for a brunch that meant we neither had to prepare breakfast nor cook lunch.

Being called The Bull, the toilets had been given quirky names in a cow style to match the name of the pub. Male toilets were labelled Bulls. Females' (with changing for babies) were Cows and Calves. All clear enough and a lot easier to understand than some other toilet labelling I have seen where you have to know symbols, Latin or about X and Y chromosomes. At The Bull, no revision is required in order to relieve yourself.

There is also a disabled loo. At this point the humour/ quirkiness of the landlord ended or he/she lost their bottle. The toilet signs read, in order: Bulls, Cows and Calves, then… Disabled. I am disabled and so entitled to use the disabled toilets. Why not label it:

Mad Cow

or

Carcasses Unfit For Human Consumption

Just because we are disabled, it does not mean we have no sense of humour.

A New Career

I had to give up being a lawyer, yet wanted to continue working. My career as rat handler and house-husband was going well. However, the scope for promotion was limited and I had not received a pay-rise since I started. Or indeed pay. So I have been considering taking the plunge and doing something else. Work that involves interaction with others is vital to me and the cash is always useful.

In my twenties, I was a teacher in a school in Lesotho (a little more on this later). I have also been a law lecturer. I love teaching and had always intended to move back to it at some point, probably close to retirement.

Well here I am. Not close to, but AT retirement and I want to teach in my final year(s). Potential employers do not like my latest CV (or 'Résumé', for American readers). It is basically my pre-cancer CV stapled to a post-operation scan image with a note simply stating:

"You do the subtraction."

Also, in interviews, how am I going to answer questions like:

"Where do you see yourself in five years' time?"

The honest answer is not exactly endearing:

"In an advanced state of decomposition"

Against these odds, I managed to get through an interview process and landed myself a position teaching soon-to-be solicitors at a university. Having handed in my house husband notice to Lu and purchased a jacket with patches on the elbow, I started work earlier this week. It's difficult beginning in a new organisation at my age, especially in a role I have not performed for decades. However, simply being in a room full of people actually listening to me makes it so fulfilling. With the family I have, it is also so unfamiliar.

Indian Takeaway Night

Last Saturday evening we got an Indian takeaway for the family using my newly acquired wages. This was partly to celebrate my law lecturing and partly to avoid having to do any cooking. We all ate together in the kitchen which is a good bonding time for us. It also avoids turmeric stains on the sofa.

At the end of the meal we make up a 'rat pot' for our furry buddies (as we always do). They always get left-overs. I wash the sauce off the chicken dhansak as I do not think it is very good for them. They also get a little piece of naan, some lentils and, of course, a piece of popadom which will have chutney stuck on it. I brought this to them in their cage. In doing so, I realised I had delivered to them an entire(rat-sized) Indian meal with all the trimmings. The only thing missing was the chocolate that comes with the bill and the hot flannel. As I delivered it, I could not help myself and had to ask them:

"What would gentlemen like to drink with the food?"

If only I had the braided waistcoat.

Career Progression

I lasted as a law lecturer for less than two weeks. I've had longer ear infections. What is more embarrassing is that I was dismissed before even delivering my first lecture. I was let go during the induction training.

It was similar to the following situation. A bloke, on paper, seems to be perfectly qualified to be a 100-metre sprinter and therefore makes the team. However, at the pre-race pep talk, he pitches up on a disability scooter eating a pizza.

Apparently, lecturers require a full brain – all of it in their head. For me, finding the lecture hall at the right time was a problem. I therefore retired without having actually met a student – other than in the lift down to reception on my way out.

This marked a watershed for me. A realisation that I can no longer perform in the professional world I used to inhabit. It's hard accepting that about yourself, but better than having it demonstrated in front of people on a daily basis.

So, with tail between legs, I have re-applied for the house-husband position at home. Lu says she is currently talking to other candidates and will get back to me. I think she is joking, but to demonstrate my usefulness, I managed to paint my son Sacha's bedroom. However, in the process of doing so, I dropped an entire tray of paint on the carpet. I therefore got sacked from this job too, even though I was working for free. I probably saved £200 by painting the walls myself and will spend £300 on buying a new carpet. So my first home pay packet was a spectacular minus one hundred pounds.

This is why I have started writing again. A smart move because, by the time people realise I am not very good at this either, they have already bought the book.

Coco Popped

Devastatingly, my pet rat Coco passed away this week. She was two-and-a-half. That's an old lady in Ratty World.

She really was one of the loveliest rats you could ever meet. Just before she departed, we took her to the vet. Rats are prone to cancer and the vet's diagnosis was that Coco had a brain tumour. Now hang on! That's just not fair!! Fate is really now starting to take the piss and, at the same time, seems to be running out of new ideas. It's like Alexander Litvinenko being informed, shortly before his death, that his pet rabbit 'Mr Nibbles' had died of polonium poisoning.

So how ominous is Coco's cause of death? The most positive way of looking at it is that Coco took the bullet for me and I'm now cured. She took the disease off me and is now my beloved scape-rat. Admittedly, the science supporting this theory is shaky. Another thought is that this is clearly ominous – that it won't be long before Lu has to take me to be put to sleep before leaving me in a pile of dead rodents and walking away with a £35 bill.

To keep my one remaining rat, Poppy, company we have adopted Beau (another rat) from friends. Beau is also lovely, if a little incontinent. Over the last year or so I have developed a skin complaint and my cheeks go itchy, scabby and red. Beau also has a series of crusty scabs around the side of her head – a bit like me with my post-operation scars and bald patches. Further evidence that people start to look like their pets and get the same ailments. Just as well that our goldfish,

Lawrence, died before I picked up fin rot. Lawrence's death was less traumatic than Coco's and he got the traditional goldfish burial at sea.

Having two rats is great but I still miss canine company. I absolutely love dogs but, as mentioned, cannot get one. Instead I spend much of my free time hanging around supermarkets petting some random canine tied up outside. None of the supermarkets, owners or dogs tend to mind and so I continue to devote time to my hobby of dogging.

Too Much Time on My Hands

Now that I am officially medically retired, I want to use whatever time I have left to help with the big issues facing humanity. I am warming up for this by addressing the following:

Issue 1 – Hygiene Certificates

Have you noticed the little hygiene certificates that restaurants proudly display in their windows? There are five circles, with one to five of them filled in with a blob to give the hygiene score. Invariably, the restaurant gets four blobs, which it boasts about by making sure you cannot enter the premises without seeing this. It is rare to see less than three blobs as, presumably, the restaurant would be too embarrassed to display it. I also cannot recall ever seeing a full five-blob rating.

I have done some research and, apparently, it is voluntary whether or not to display this certification. With a four-blob rating, why is it that these establishments are so proud of the fact that twenty percent of basic hygiene procedures have not been met? I would change the law so that displaying the certification is compulsory and the establishment must, in the absence of a five-blob rating, give the reason for dropping blobs. A typical rating would read something like this:

● ● ● ● *Good basic food hygiene; surfaces clear and regularly cleaned; consumables all fresh and in date; no rubbish left lying around; no visible sign of vermin but the chef sometimes does a poo without washing his hands.*

Issue 2 – Fragranced Baby Wipes

I understand the convenience of baby wipes – all absorbent, soft, moist and immediately ready for use. Perfect, when running water is not available, for removing unwanted remnants from your cute offspring's soft bottom. Or, in the case of my children, bottom, lower back, upper back, neck and hair. And, in one case, the formerly white wall of a nice restaurant in Cadiz. However, why do most brands of baby-wipes have a fragranced variant? In fact, fragranced is the default and one must seek out the non-fragranced product. Ask any mother and they will confirm, babies smell lovely. They just do. A perfume spray for application to babies would be unthinkable. So why do we want our perfect little cherub to smell of artificial flowers or meadows? More specifically, why do we want *those* parts of a baby to smell of flowers or meadows? Anyway, what are you doing smelling my baby *there*? Indeed, why am I encouraging you with enticing odours to smell my baby *there*? Forget 'Lemon Fresh', 'Summer Meadows' and 'Pine'. There should be only one fragrance available and that should be 'Not Shit'.

Issue 3 – Pillow Cases

Pillow cases should be cotton, white and completely flat (i.e. no designs that are in relief and no patterns or decoration other than printed ones). The whole point about pillows and, by extension, pillow cases, is that they are there for comfort. That is their purpose. During the day they are covered by a bed spread or duvet. At night it is dark and one tends to have eyes shut. Appearance is irrelevant or, at very most, secondary to comfort. Any three-dimensional design that in any way protrudes ends up in negative form on your face in the morning. As you get older, the length of time it remains increases. At my age, it is possible that the sun has set before the imprint is gone. This is where my wonderful mother-in-law, Joan comes in. Now Joan is the perfect in-law. Generous, kind, spoils me rotten and thinks the sun shines out of my back side. We love our trips to Brighton to see Grandma Joan and Grandpa David and do these as often as we can. Joan does have one failing though – pillow cases. Joan uses pillow cases with a pleated striped design. I repeat: pleated. Now that is well and truly three dimensional – it stands out (or in) from the surface of the main part of the material. From the use of this pillow case alone, Joan can tell how well or badly I slept. She can even tell at what angle I slept. She knows I have had a terrible night if there are loads of creases in all directions on all surfaces of my head. And a great night's sleep results in a perfect indent on the side of my face showing two, deeply engrained and totally parallel lines together with a leaf.

This takes me back to the time when I fell asleep at my parents' house on their sofa. My parents, Sue and Barry, have these ornate, Persian-style cushions. I woke up to find a perfect indent of a sequin elephant on my forehead.

*

Apart from solving World problems such as these, I spend much of my day doing crosswords with a pet rat on my shoulder. I argue that this is to keep my brain active and to stop it turning into mush (the crossword is meant to do that, not the rat). I only have half a brain, so it seems sensible to give the remaining half as much exercise as possible.

Economising

There is also the financial challenge of my retirement to deal with. We do not starve with myself not working but date nights have become quite modest affairs. I need to feel I am contributing to the household financially, so I have started an economy drive:

- My weekly date night with Lu provides an opportunity to save a load of money on babysitters by going one at a time, then catching up on conversation and discussing the food when the second of us returns.
- During grocery shopping, instead of buying expensive meat, why not harvest road kill? How bad can hedgehog crumble be? Also, a run over squirrel makes an ideal sandwich filler which, in flat form, is almost the perfect shape for immediate use in a ciabatta. The tail may need some pruning though.
- You may have heard of the theoretical ever-lasting light bulb or razor blade. Well how about the bottle of mouthwash that never runs out? This one tip could ruin Listerine's business model. Quite simply, when you have swished the mouthwash around your mouth for the desired time, do not spit it out into the sink or toilet. Instead, spit it back into the bottle. I cannot actually claim that the mouthwash will last an infinite amount of time (despite having just suggested this). Don't forget, some of the mouthwash must adhere to the teeth and mouth (otherwise how would the minty taste stay around for a while?). I am just saying that money can be

saved by making the bottle last, say, five years. Do not worry about the possibility of shared germs. After all it kills 99.9% of all known bacteria and viruses (or perhaps that is the toilet cleaner?). My recommendation is that you do change bottles every five years or when the mouthwash starts to get chewy, whichever happens first. Certainly change it when it gets crunchy.

- When ordering take away for the family, do not pay for the drinks to be delivered. Why pay restaurant prices for drinks when you have a fridge with beer and a couple of bottles of wine on the go? And for the children/teetotallers in your life, use this trick I came up with recently. We were all out of soda, so the kids gave their various drink orders for me to pick up whilst the curry-mobile was on its way, varying in colour from fluorescent orange to light blue. Then I walked past our local budget supermarket and had a brainwave. Rather than buying various small bottles or cans of different fizzy drinks with the arguments this will cause, why not buy one enormous budget bottle of diet lemonade that everyone dislikes equally? No arguments. You can get three litres of the stuff, it has no sugar and it costs £1.

Everyone's a winner

Well I am. I'm drinking craft beer. "Everyone's a winner", I repeat – that is until you think about it in a little more detail. The price of these three litres of pop is just £1. That is significantly cheaper than the supermarket's own brand equivalent sized bottle of still water. Not mountain spring water from the

Highlands of Scotland, nor from some Brecon Valley stream. Not even carbonated. Just water. This bottled tap water is more expensive than my diet lemonade, and probably nicer too. Now hang on! Think about it. Lemonade/Diet Lemonade is drinkable water that they add stuff to like carbon dioxide, flavourings, sweeteners and (dare I wish for this?) lemons. How can they make this stuff cheaper than the equivalent volume of water which, one presumes (or at least hopes), is the starting point? This suggests one of two possibilities:

1) They start with something cheaper than drinkable water. Enough said.
2) They start with drinkable water yet add something to it that makes the water less valuable. To emphasise:

A liquid less valuable than water.

From a different perspective, they are using the liquid to dump chemicals which would otherwise cost money to dispose of.

My son, Jonah, had a response which was more reassuring. Basically look at the people buying these drinks. People who buy bottled water, when the same stuff comes out of your tap at home for free, are generally middle class Muswell Hill types who have a bit of money in their hipster trousers. The mark up is greater for the water because the type of person buying water must be easier to get extra money out of. I hope he is right as I still have two-and-three-quarter litres to get through.

Spring 2017

Beau Hoo

It's early March and my adopted rat Beau just passed away having reached a very old age. We asked the original owners if they would like to come to the funeral. They could not as they were away but wanted to see the body to pay their last respects. Unable to visit for a good few days, we had a dilemma. Apparently, the original owners had a similar quandary themselves some years back when the rat they were looking after for someone else passed away on their watch. They solved this quandary by freezing the dead rat – yes, in their kitchen freezer! Nobody loves rats more than I do but even I would not have gone this far. Anyway, the owners did not collect it and, as is typical with things going in freezers, they soon forgot it was there. When they had their next freezer clear out, they spent an age trying to figure out what food they had bought in that shape (the tail was sticking out straight). There you go: one freaky Halloween popsicle to turn the tables on even the hardiest trick-or-treater.

*

To help us all (but especially me) with these rodent bereavements, we decided to buy three new boy rats – who were brothers. We didn't really want that many, but the shop insisted we took all three because they were family. When it comes to rats, I have a very low threshold for guilt. There was also another person in the shop interested in buying them and I was unnerved by the rather odd name they intended to use:

Snake Meal, April 2017

So we took the plunge and purchased the whole batch.

Two of the three are absolutely lovely and adore human company.

However, the third rat does not have the charm of the other two. He suffers from severe incontinence. Either that or he likes to mark his territory. This rat crouches there with hunched ratty shoulders scrabbling around and shitting on me. He also has a Jewish nose. So I named him Hershel, partly because that is a traditional Yiddish name and partly because Grumpyshitebag is more of a mouthful. I can really relate to Hershel.

Right now, London is in the middle of unseasonably warm weather – almost a heatwave. I make sure the room is nicely aired and that they have a big bowl of water to drink and play in. I went into the rat-room/study yesterday and found Hershey perched on the edge of the water bowl, in a sort of heat-induced trance, with his balls submerged in the water (rats, male rats that is, do have large, protruding testicles). Whilst the other boys are far more charming and loving to humans, if I were a rat, I would be Hershel, cooling off my balls in the communal drinking water. This should be a warning to anybody sharing a drinking fountain with me during hot weather.

The School Run is a Walk

I take my daughter Thea to school most days. A nice fifteen-minute walk through the woods with my seven-year-old.

On the way we play various games. We've progressed from I-Spy and today I taught her mental noughts and crosses. Basically just playing the game but in our heads. This has big advantages because, not only does it save on paper, you can play it anywhere you like. It also means that the two of us can be crosses, which is both of our preference. You can play either by description of position (top middle, bottom left hand corner etc.) or referencing a phone keypad (so middle right is 6, bottom left 7 and so on). Apparently there are some people mentally agile enough to play chess in this manner. I am not that clever – certainly since I had Pear removed a couple of years ago. Mental chess is way out of my league. However, mental noughts and crosses is fairly easy and I won two-nil (not that I am a competitive dad).

Such games are about finding the right level to stretch your brain (or what's left of it, in my case) without overwhelming it. In the end, we found the perfect mental game for playing verbally together whilst walking to school: mental Hungry Hippos. Our conversation changed from:

"Top right. That's a line – the right-hand column!"

to

"Snap, snap, snap, snap SNAP! I won!!"

I advise against mental Kerplunk. When Thea took out the imaginary green straw on the top left, to me it was clear that all the marbles (bar one or two) would fall, whereas Thea thought none had fallen. I suppose she is only seven and has not yet developed the perception skills of an adult.

Another game we play on our walk to school is:

Animal, Vegetable or Mineral

The person whose turn it is has to think of something and the other(s) has to establish what it is with questions that have only yes/no answers. The only clue given is whether it is an animal, vegetable (i.e. plant) or mineral (i.e. never been living). I like to throw a curveball with an item like 'mushroom' which, according to my biology 'O' level, is none of these. Lu also plays when she can join us and has to do the very difficult ones. Last time was sheer genius on my part – Lu picked 'Determinism' which I got in three guesses starting only with it being none of animal, mineral or vegetable.

First Guess: "*A concept?*"

Lu: "*Yes.*"

Second Guess: "*Is it Nihilism?*"

Lu: "*Staggeringly close*" (well, to a non-philosopher – falling in the category of philosophical stuff – probably).

Third Guess: "*Is it Determinism?*"

On Monday, when I alone will take Thea to school, I am going to see how she does with 'Incredulity' and 'Jurisprudence'.

For today though, we played a completely new game. It does not have a name but is based upon making theoretical, binary choices.

Question 1:

"Would you rather have the ability to fly or to turn invisible?"

Easy one to start. The correct answer (according to both of us) is fly. Flying must be inexhaustibly fun and has always been one of my fantasies. Invisibility? You would scare a few people in supermarkets. Maybe a bit of revenge on people who have caused you grief over the years. I am not saying that I wouldn't be busy with my invisibility. It's just that flying would keep me occupied longer and in a more wholesome way.

Question 2:

"Would you rather your father was Lord Voldemort or Donald Trump?"

Tricky. People would hate you less as the descendant of the Dark Lord, yet with Trump as your Dad, you would have loads of money. Answer: Voldemort.

Finally:

"Would you prefer that your face looked like your bum or that your bum looked like your face? (if they look different in the first place)"

I am assuming that this question means 'properly look like' not just passing resemblance. So a cleft chin is not enough. Thea's point was that more people see your face than your bum, so the answer must be a face-bum and not a bum-face. A reassuring answer that is based upon sound logic in respect of people who are not porn stars.

I love this time walking to school and back with Thea. It gives me a proper chance to catch up with her without the constant distractions of screens and other electronics. However, a tricky situation arose last week when I was posed with one of those questions all parents dread:

"Daddy, What's the F word?"

Help! Where's Lu when I really need her? I tried fobbing her off with 'Fiddlesticks' but she's way too clever for that. Another tactic:

"But there are lots of F words you know, such as 'fish' and 'finger' and, of course, 'fishfinger'."

The real problem is that I know lots of rude F words. It is a balance between honesty and openness on the one hand, and not teaching her new obscenities (ones she was not seeking) on the other. Playing this out in my half-brain, I could anticipate imminent disaster. We are open-minded and my children have friends parented by single sex couples. So I considered giving this response:

"You know if one man loves another man in the way Mummy and Daddy love each other? You know, like little Ollie and his two daddies. Daddy One and Daddy Two love each other very dearly. They might do special cuddles that are private. One of these special cuddles is called 'fisting'. That's an F word. Now what are you doing at school today?"

Fortunately, the sudden appearance of an entertaining squirrel meant the question was forgotten.

*

On the walk home, I always take Thea a snack. It needs to be high energy but ideally, not sugary. What about a nice apple or pear? Parents reading this will know what a fantasy this is. Fruit would be accepted by my daughter in the same way a cat owner has to accept a mauled mouse.

My favourite snack to take her is monkey nuts i.e. peanuts in the shell. Natural, with no added sugar or salt. The down side is that they must be smuggled into school and not eaten until well off the grounds. Owing to today's improved allergy awareness, schools treat the taking in of anything containing nuts as worse than bringing in yellow cake uranium. I had no idea how dangerous peanuts are. I foolishly considered them only a minor choking hazard for baby birds. Instead they are an evil product that is just waiting to be weaponised. So poor Thea will have to make do with fruit. Until that is identified as a biohazard as well.

Volunteering

To fill in the time between school runs and washing cycles (as well as to give 'something back'), I have decided to take on some voluntary work. In particular, I would love to work with animals. My perfect role would be to work for an animal charity and be their Chief Puppy Cuddler. That must be the best job ever and I would pay to do it. Surely even I could not get sacked from that? I must have a chance of getting a voluntary position – yes? In fact, no. I phoned around and could find nothing – there were no positions vacant. Some lucky sod had already nicked my unpaid job.

Apparently there was even a waiting list. A waiting list for providing free work? I cannot understand this. How can any organisation, charitable or profit-making, decline free labour? They are effectively saying:

"Thank you for your interest in our organisation. However, us engaging you on a zero hours contract to clean up dog crap, with no employment rights for you (and with no pay at all) would cause detriment to us. You working for us actually reduces the value of our organisation. Thanks, but no thanks."

I don't get it. Basically, I cannot even give myself away.

*

After several months of such rejections, I finally managed to land a voluntary job in a Muswell Hill soup kitchen.

Every Sunday evening I go to the hall in a nearby church. It is open five times a week, but I only do a single evening shift each week. My main task is to ladle out the soup (prepared in advance by one of the chefs) and to chat with the guests. I have therefore been selected for front of house duties, which I am quite chuffed about. Other volunteers spend the hour scrubbing pans.

Everybody is welcome. There are no checks or registers. Many guests are not actually homeless – we don't check. But all are, in one way or another, down on their luck.

The guests get a bowl of soup (or two if they want it) and a main course. There will be a meat one and a vegetarian option. There may be a pudding too. Usually cake. This is dependent upon what the bakeries have kindly donated that week.

The soup is always vegetarian (as are many of the clientele). Usually mixed vegetables and a variety of beans and pulses. Always very nourishing, despite such cheap ingredients.

So the guests get a bowl of soup, a main course (including vegetarian alternative), tea and a nice civilised environment. This is enhanced by some wonderful musicians who donate their time to giving the hall an amazing atmosphere.

One day, the chef was away and I did some cooking. A giant chilli to feed up to forty people. It was pretty good, despite the meat not being freshly ground, organic, free-range Wagyu steak. To my relief given the time it took me to make the chilli, the vegetarian alternative had already been prepared. It looked like pasta with vegetables. Most of the ingredients would have been given out by local supermarkets for free (which is very kind of them).

I also do the less glamorous side of the work such as stacking chairs, washing up and mopping floors. We volunteers muck in with whatever needs doing.

This work does give me satisfaction and I enjoy it. The best part, though, is being able to casually mention it at social occasions:

"Yes, I do a little volunteering at a soup kitchen. What do you do as your contribution to society?"

I deliver this with all the fake modesty I can muster. I had no idea how deliciously enjoyable self-righteousness could be. In fact, now I think about it, I can stop my voluntary work and just phrase my condescending comments in the past tense. Or just lie. It is not as if my friends and family are going to check.

I am also acutely aware that I am just one roll of fate's dice away from being the other side of the serving table at the soup kitchen. Let's see how the finances go.

⁂

On the whole, the guests at the soup kitchen are lovely. Friendly, intelligent and appreciative people who just seem to have taken a wrong turn somewhere along the way. Or had some pretty appalling luck doled out to them – I can relate to that.

There is, though, one bloke at the soup kitchen who seems to take some pleasure in verbally abusing me. He's not the first person in my life to do this. However, it is rather annoying as I have willingly given up my time to help him. I would cheerily approach him and say:

"Hello there. How are you doing and can I bring you more soup?" He chirpily responds:

"No. Fuck off and leave me alone. I want to be by myself."

I cannot get too upset with him. Firstly, I am told his brain has been seriously messed up by drugs and alcohol. I get this. My brain has been seriously messed up by radiotherapy which is far less enjoyable than drugs, so I did not even get the up side there. Secondly, if somebody invited me in, then fed and served me I would not say to them:

"Fuck off and leave me alone. Just let me eat."

Call me an etiquette freak if you will, but I just would not say this. However, I might be *thinking* this. So perhaps we are quite similar, and he is just more honest and open than I am.

Household Appliances

Even with my new-found human and rodent itinerary, I still have time for other activities. My favourite is arguing with department stores. In particular, in relation to those ten-hour appointment slots you are forced to accept. They drive me crazy.

When our brand new dishwasher goes wrong after its very first use I ring up the store to complain. They can get somebody round but their arrival will be any time between 8.00am and 6.00pm on Wednesday next week.

What kind of business is it where the company can only predict the whereabouts of its employees within a window of ten hours? Even mountain rescue staff must radio ahead where they will be and what their estimated timing is. Do the delivery staff of department stores really only commit to starting their shift at some point during daylight hours?

For my second appointment (or third, or fourth), when the appliance in question has repeatedly failed to work, I inform the shop that the ten-hour delivery slot is not convenient to me. I should not be forced to take a day off work to wait in for them again (I would of course be home all day tending rodents, but it's the principle of the matter). It's their fault for selling me a dodgy appliance. I try explaining this to the poor sod who has the misfortune to take my call. When asked to wait at home ten hours for a visit to put things right, my reply never alters and is along the following lines:

"I am quite busy that day what with school runs and shopping, but I will try to be home to meet your delivery and installation team. I do not know exactly when I will be home but if your team would please wait for me on my porch, I should be home some time between 1.00pm and 7.00pm. Perhaps the members of the delivery and installation team could each take a day's annual leave to do this for me?"

Apparently, department stores have no sense of irony.

*

This arguing with big businesses came to a head recently. We had to replace our enormous American-style fridge-freezer. The delivery guys from the online supplier were actually very good indeed and had to do all sorts of jiggery pokery to get this massive appliance through our narrow house. In the process of disassembling and reassembling, they managed to leave one of the heads/bits from their electronic screwdriver in the new fridge. I only discovered this after the team had departed. If this were my screwdriver set, I would find it very frustrating to have one of the heads missing. So I did the decent thing and phoned up the supplier on its customer helpline:

Me: *"Here's my order number."*

Supplier: *"Thank you. How can I help you, Mr Blain?"*

Me: *"You can't. I have phoned to help you; in fact to help your delivery team."*

Supplier: *"What seems to be the problem?"*

Me: *"No problem as such. Just your team left some bit of kit in my fridge. I'd like to return it to them."*

Supplier: *"Is there a problem with the appliance then, Sir?"*

Me: *"No. Other than the very minor problem of a screwdriver head being in my egg compartment reducing its capacity by approximately one egg. Not a problem as such, though. The fridge is otherwise working fine."*

Supplier: *"I am sorry about that. So how can we help you?"*

Me: *"You can't. I have phoned to help you."*

Supplier: *"I'm sorry but we can't provide that kind of service."*

Me: *"What kind of service? I don't want any service."*

Supplier (in frustration): *"I'm sorry but we are here to offer help. That is what our helpline is for."*

Me: *"So you confirm that this is a customer helpline, yes?"*

Supplier: *"Yes"*

Me: *"Well I am a customer trying to help. Of all the options available on the automated system that eventually put me through to you, Customer Helpline seemed the closest to the mark. My situation involves help (albeit offered by me, not to me) and I am a customer. I patiently listened to all the options and there wasn't a single one for delivery team leaving tool parts in an egg department of a fridge. I checked – twice."*

Supplier: *"We can only help customers on this line. Not the other way round."*

Me: "*Well can you give me the number for the customer helpline where it is the customer offering help?*"

Supplier: "*We don't have one of those. So how can I help you?*"

Me: [Big sigh] "*If your rules say that it is YOU that must provide the help, then you can help me by posting me a stamped addressed envelope, sturdy enough not to let the bit fall out.*"

Supplier: "*Where do you want it addressed to?*"

Me: "*The outer envelope? Me of course.*"

Supplier: "*No, the other one.*"

Me: "*I don't care. That's up to you. I would think the home or work address of the bloke who owns the electronic screwdriver would be a good starting point.*"

Supplier: "*Sorry, we can't do that. However, if you are able to wait in, we can get a delivery team round for a slot tomorrow. I am prioritising this and marking it urgent. Please wait in between 8.00am and 4.00pm*"

Me: "*Are you taking the piss? So you can send a huge lorry round with three burly blokes to pick up a tiny item which is basically valueless but you can't send me an envelope? Your website claims that you pride yourselves on your efficiency. And why the hell is it urgent? I have looked after this bit for two days now and really, it is no trouble at all. In fact, my wife and I have gone out and left the bit completely unsupervised. We came home and there was no harm to it and it hadn't run rampage round our house unscrewing stuff. It really is no trouble whatsoever. Tell you what though: I'll leave it under the flower pot in our front garden and your team can collect it whenever they like."*

Supplier: *"I am sorry, Sir, but it is our strict policy to insist that somebody is in whenever we make a collection."*

Me: *"I tell you what. I will take the risk. In the event that anyone rummages through our front garden in the hope of assembling components for a tool kit, then miraculously finds it and steals it, I will buy your guys a new one. I'm sticking my neck out here for you. Just the other day, a burglar was going through next door's rose garden looking for an eighth of an inch masonry drill bit."*

Supplier: *"Sorry sir, we can't accept that. Company policy."*

Me: *"You have a policy on screwdriver bits left in fridges by your delivery teams? If this happens so frequently as to require its own policy, what does that policy say should happen in this situation?"*

Supplier: *"To my knowledge it has not happened before."*

Me: *"So your firm went to the effort of creating and implementing a policy for a scenario that has never, to your knowledge, occurred prior to today. Although, to be fair, my last workplace had a fire policy and it never burnt down."*

Supplier: *"So shall I book you in for tomorrow from eight until four?"*

Me: *"No, bugger off. I've assuaged any remnants of guilt I had. And this call alone has cost me more than the value of the item."*

Anyway, the long and short of all this is that I now have a spare part to an electronic screwdriver with no device to put it in.

*

I also use my time valuably by naming our kitchen appliances and furniture. When I say naming, I do not mean stating that it is a fridge or oven etc. I mean giving the appliance a real name so that it feels like part of the family. Our kitchen table is called Mable (kind of obvious). The fridge, discussed in detail above, is called Fredge. The oven has two parts and so, two names. After all, if you had conjoined twins they would each get their own name. So the bottom half with the actual oven bit is called Owen and the top, eye-level part is called Bear. Think about it – who do you know named Bear that is not actually a bear?

I do not generally name other things (apart from children and pets). However, a previous car was called Rafjee which is more or less the number plate if you remove the numbers and add a couple of vowels. Our last car should have been called 'Czs' but I don't know how to pronounce this. Possibly a Czech version of 'Chas'? Maybe the chassis number will give me something to work with.

Baking Bad

I doubt this counts as a hobby, but I have this 'thing' where I have to correct grammar and punctuation. I do not particularly enjoy doing this. It's just something I do as a form of compulsion. I will do this on chalk boards and notices. However, my favourite is correcting the grammar and spelling of teachers' comments that appear on a child's work displayed on a classroom wall. Well, they can hardly complain. I always take a red biro along to parents' evenings for these purposes.

I have also taken up baking bread (using a bread machine, of course). The first few loaves were a bit of a disaster. My sunflower loaf had the consistency, density and taste of plasticine. Not enough yeast. My white bloomer had the consistency and density of candy-floss although, sadly, not the taste. Too much yeast.

With plenty of time on my hands, I like to make a game out of things or turn them into a fantasy. When making bread, I pretend that I am not in my kitchen. Instead, I am working in an illegal narcotics lab. Maybe an urban meth kitchen. Before starting, I line up all the ingredients. I take the packet of flour, stab the side of it with a knife and rub a little of the white powder into my gum before nodding my approval and stating:

"Yeh – good shit."

When Lu comes home I have left a few small lines of flour on the counter together with a rolled-up twenty-pound note.

Film Night

Lu and I enjoy a film together. A couple of hours, curling up next to each other to see if I can work out what the hell is going on in the film's plot. I am terrible at following a film and its twists. This goes way back before my misfortunes struck. I am endlessly mocked by my friends for losing the thread of *Carry on up the Khyber* by going to get a beer at a critical moment. Now, being Pear-less, it is utterly hopeless to even try.

Lu and I usually have a similar taste in films, if not identical. I can usually work out if I am going to enjoy the film by the caption at the top of the film review, next to the star rating (measured out of five like the blob hygiene ratings of restaurants). That single sentence, taking a few seconds to read, will determine quite accurately, how much I will enjoy it. This should come as no surprise as it is the job of the reviewer. In fact, I do not need to read the whole review. Just the summary. A description starting:

'A maverick alien-killing superhero in a fast car is out for revenge...'

probably relates to a right corker of a film. It will mesmerise me and bore the socks off Lu. If the film's description commences:

'A woman's journey...'

then it is not for me.

However, this time saving technique (of not reading the whole review) can have drawbacks. One of our staying in movie nights involved her selecting the film from our satellite directory. She picked one which, to my complete surprise, was very sad indeed. I have enough 'sad' in my life right now and do not want any more, particularly when I am not prepared for it. I initially agreed to watch it because it sounded pretty raunchy; a kind of erotic fantasy for adult only viewing. Certainly not sad. I thought my luck was in. This conclusion came from reading the summary of the review:

'An eye-popping movie that should not be missed, clearly aimed at a male audience. Do not attempt to watch it without a box of tissues.'

Photography

At this point, I should mention Lu's hobbies – one of which I find particularly morbid. Lu is going a bit mad taking photos of me and videoing me. All the time, in all places and with various combinations of children and rats.

"That all sounds very nice!"

I hear you cry out.

"What's wrong with that?"

It is terrible – I hate it. I never used to be the subject of so many photographs because I do not make a particularly nice picture. Now, with the constant clicking of a phone camera, I feel like Kate Middleton in a short skirt, climbing out of the back seat of a car. Lu wants the pictures to remember me by and to help the kids remember me when I snuff it. To myself, and for that reason, each photo is a reminder of my imminent departure from this world. I can just imagine Lu talking the kids through the photos and videos a few years post-Adam:

"That one is Daddy looking for his keys."

"There's Dad, utterly helpless, whilst he tries to find his phone."

"Here he is! Lost in our own back garden. Isn't he funny?"

"Look – there's your Daddy swearing at the lawnmower!"

And so on. This snapping away is another constant reminder that the Big C has the upper hand and is just biding its time before flexing its muscles again.

I try to frustrate this photography. Whenever a picture is being taken, I act as dead as possible. Like the morbid subjects of Victorian memorial portraiture. Usually eyes half shut, vacant expression and tongue lolling out. If sitting down, I sprawl and do not support my head. If standing up, I try to look as if I am being propped up. Eyes, if open, must look as vacant as possible. Hopefully the pictures will be printed in sepia to give the full effect.

*

Lu's paparazzi behaviour seems to increase as scan day approaches and today was results day.

Sitting in the waiting area of the hospital, I began to notice people were giving me strange looks. Certainly more than usual. After a good ten minutes of this, I was called in to see my consultant. She gave a double take when she saw me and frowned. This could not be good news. Except it was:

Another Clear Scan!

Before this news had sunk in, she then proceeded to ask:

"How are you doing in yourself Adam? Are there any personal issues you would like to discuss?"

I responded:

"Well, other than a small rash, I'm doing fine in the circumstances."

To which she replied:

"That's good to hear but are you aware you have white powder around your nostrils?"

After five minutes of red-cheeked explanation, I left really not sure I had convinced her it was flour from my morning's narcotics lab make-believe.

New Car

I had to surrender my driving licence when I got ill. However, by surviving this long, I have got it back on condition I don't have any kind of seizures (whether or not driving at the time). I do my absolute best to remain seizure-free and so far, have been successful.

Shortly after my re-licensing, our old car finally died on us. It was a big, clunky seven-seater diesel that sounded like a tractor. We therefore blew our savings on a new hybrid car that is very environmentally friendly. You put a tiny drop of fuel in the car and it glides along mostly powered by self-satisfaction or something. I say it is environmentally friendly, but that is on the premise that one has to have a car. I still walk or bus it nearly everywhere but we do need a car, primarily for Lu's work.

I find it very difficult to use this new car. For starters it has no slot for a key. Instead you have a little cup-holder in which you place the keys. Just put the keys in the hole. The whole set, including front door key and the key for the padlock to the shed. Stick them all in and the car sorts it out for you and chooses which key to listen to.

There are two brakes, both operated by foot. So the hand brake is actually a foot brake but so is the normal brake. To activate the car, you have to press various buttons and pedals in the correct order. It is not intuitive at all. There is no big green button which is labelled 'Go'. I have just about got the hang of it now, so long as nothing complicated arises like rain or darkness.

If you follow the news, you will see that these hybrid vehicles are never used by robbers as a get-away car. I can see why:

"Quick Shorty, get in the car. Coppers are coming!"

"OK, let me just take my coffee out of the coffee holder and replace it with keys. Now I'll press the power button whilst pressing the brake. Oops, wrong brake.... I've done that, but forgotten to press the 'P' button whatever that is. Hang on, wing mirrors aren't out. Oh look – windscreen wiper fluid is running low. And you, Muscles, haven't got your seat belt on. Radio 3 keeps coming on through the Satnav. [presses more buttons]. No, I cannot go faster. Anyway, if I go too fast we will stop achieving maximum fuel economy. Ah, I'm in reverse – that was why it was bleeping. Wow, in the display I can see the whole world from the perspective of my exhaust pipe."

Signs of Ageing

One thing I am really feeling since diagnosis is the ageing process and its constant progression. In fact, acceleration. All the unpleasant parts of getting old have to be squeezed into my abridged life.

I am fully aware of the cosmetics advert's Seven Signs of Ageing but feel they are totally wrong and inappropriate to most blokes having their mid-life crises. Yes, the greyness, aching back, knees and nasal hair all continue but here are the real Seven Signs of Ageing, which are becoming ever more familiar to me:

1) Flirting with women. Most straight men do it at any age post-puberty. However, there is a precise point in time for every man in a relationship that highlights his decline. The situation is where you flirt with another woman in the presence of your wife/partner. Of course your other half is cross early on in the relationship and when you are youngish! However, there is a point some time in middle age, where this changes. The looks of annoyance from one's better half are replaced by looks of hilarity. The look used to be an implied: '*What are you doing? I own you!*'
   This changes to a look implying: '*As if!!*'

2) Saying really stupid things. There are, of course, the various noises we start to make when getting in/out of a chair or if (perish the thought) we have to crouch down. Furthermore, I have started making very strange noises when I yawn. A bit like a Wookiee in pain. But we actually say stupid

things in whole sentences as well as making ridiculous noises when we age. For example, a pet rat's favourite place is somewhere that is warm, dark, dry, comfortable and (ideally) smelling of humans. Consequently, my rat Coco loved burrowing into peoples' clothes whilst they were being worn. With this information in mind, consider the following. I went to a party, where I met an attractive woman. She was particularly buxom, wearing a very low cut and revealing dress. Her cleavage was mesmerising. However, the combination of middle age and cancer have made me totally dull and sexless. So I didn't think twice about pointing down her cleavage and proclaiming:
"My rat, Coco, would just love it in there."

The important thing to appreciate here is that I have had part of my brain removed. Therefore, my advice to people in my situation is to plan (in what's left of your brain) what you intend to say, before saying it out loud. You then have an opportunity to change it to something more suave and sexy. For example, I could have said:

"You know I'm not the only one in my household who would really appreciate your tits."

Then gradually edge the conversation over to rats. Far less creepy.

3) Striving to be more efficient when it comes to any form of physical exertion. The best example of this is picking things up off the floor or trying to avoid it. A couple of tips: (i) Don't put things on the floor in the first place. If you

have to put something down and a surface is not available, use the stairs (stairs you are at the bottom of obviously). About fourth one up is best. This way you only have to bend a little.

(ii) If you actually have to reach as far as the floor, at least use the opportunity to do another task whilst you are down there. Pick up something else or peel off a raisin that has been mashed into the carpet by one of the offspring.

4) Changing bodily functions. When younger and one goes for a pee there is a definite start and end to the process. Start, pee, finish. Easy enough to explain. As you get older, there is still a beginning to the urination process. It is the ending that becomes blurred. You no longer have that precise finish. The full stop, if you will. It just kind of tails out, well beyond the time of departing from the bathroom. Why are we not taught about this at school? We all know about grey hair and wrinkles.

5) The Gaping Period. This is my most reliable indicator of ageing. Suppose you are going to the toilet for a, ahem, 'proper' visit (or any visit if you are a girl), with a view to showering immediately thereafter. A sensible and logical part of a day's routine. Anyone would agree that there is no point in pulling up and buttoning/zipping up one's trousers only to take them off a few moments later. Basic common sense and prevention of needless physical exertion (see above). Leave the trousers gaping. Just gaping. Not round the ankles – a clear tripping hazard. What if the phone goes

or you need an urgent cup of tea during the Gaping Period? You're alone apart from members of your household. A decade ago, I would have made myself decent. Now, I continue with the 'gaping' for these short tasks, knowing that I will shortly be removing my trousers for a shower. As you get older, you gain confidence and care less about appearance (well I do). You gradually take on bigger and bigger tasks for the Gaping Period. You know you are getting old when you are willing to carry out a certain task during the Gaping Period. It is when you answer the door in this state. No longer caring, or perhaps forgetting that you care (and have left your trousers open). This is a cruel point in one's life; around the time that we realise that we males have turned into our fathers. I already walk around the house in my underpants, carrying a portable radio playing BBC Radio 4 on full volume. It is the middle-aged, middle-class equivalent of walking the streets with a ghetto blaster on one's shoulder. However, instead of rap coming out of the speakers, it is *Gardeners' Question Time* – and people claim that I am not 'hip'!

6) My next indicator of ageing: I have this very dry, flaky skin on my face – particularly either side of my nose. Like some old people get, although I do not yet have the red, veiny, bulbous nose. So the penultimate sign of ageing is excessive faceruff.

7) Finally, you know you are old when you start reading the obituaries and looking for people around your age. If the word 'tragedy' does not appear, then you are old.

I am literally watching the ageing process unfold before my eyes because of what I have been through. Not like a normal person where old age creeps up on them gradually over sixty years or so. I wake up each morning, look down and think:

"What's going wrong with me today?"

Then I think back to my diagnosis, three years ago almost to the day, and how I would have bitten my surgeon's hand off to have these issues. However bad my deterioration is, the process is significantly kinder to me than decomposition would be.

Holidays

Lu and I have decided that, whilst we should generally economise for the future, the holiday budget would be largely unaffected.

Our last holiday was based very much around a swimming pool. The pool lifeguards had T-shirts with a message on:

'Lifeguard. Here to keep you safe'

This got me wondering whether we should all be forced to wear T-shirts stating our job and a brief description of what it entails. For example:

'Fireman. Here to put out fires'

or

'Doctor. Here to delay your death'

or

'Corporate Lawyer. Here to ensure business documentation and transactions are compliant with company law legislation and related case law (subject to terms, restrictions, disclaimers and limitations contained within the firm's terms and conditions, copies of which are available upon request)'

I have discovered that even people in my position can get insurance for these trips. Alright, I am only covered for fire and theft, but I thought I was uninsurable.

*

Departure day arrived and we excitedly made our way to the airport in the self-satisfaction-powered car. Here is a tough one though: What to do at an airport having advised the airline of my disability? Airlines treat disability in a binary fashion. There are non-disabled people, who are herded around and kept waiting in uncomfortable plastic chairs (if any are left – otherwise it is the floor). Then there are disabled people who get a wheelchair. Nothing else. There is no smaller adjustment for people who are dying, but fairly slowly, and are reasonably fit in the meantime. The only adjustment I need is not to sit next to anyone too annoying on the flight. A free bag of nuts would also go down well.

The airport staff know immediately that I am not a seasoned wheelchair user. My fifteen-year-old son Jonah elects himself as my handler. Then it is full speed races round the terminal at sprinting pace, much of which is done as a wheelie. He beats all the other wheelchairs, gets some exercise and both of us get an adrenaline rush. This makes me worried about my next flight as I am sure my wheelchair locomotion will progress to performing jumps. That is surely what the ramps are for? I just hope his aim is only to jump a single piece of luggage.

The really difficult part of the airport experience is when I get out of the wheel chair and try to continue looking disabled. Despite being able to walk perfectly, I drag one leg along behind me and try to look exhausted (the latter being easy enough). If I forget this, I have my family there as back up to jump up and shout:

"It's a miracle!"

Summer 2017

Well This is New

Life had been plodding along quite nicely for some months. It was time for fate to move me to the top of its inbox. So, to stop any complacency on my part, I got a headache. Headaches are bad news for GBM victims. I had a headache at the very beginning of all this and it was one of the red flags that led to my ultimate diagnosis.

As long as it is just a normal headache, everything should be fine I told myself. We all get headaches and the vast majority of them are not brain cancer.

Just a headache. Like when your spectacles have the wrong prescription, or you have been staring at a screen too long. A paracetamol should take the edge off it. It doesn't. Must be a duff batch from the pharmacy.

The next day the headache was still there. Hot day. It must be dehydration. I started to worry but I had only just had a scan, so it couldn't be a new Pear. He cannot reincarnate that quickly, even with an exponential growth rate.

The third day arrived. Headache still there, especially when I cough. Probably nothing. Loads of people have three-day headaches. I thought I would confirm this by ringing a few friends as a quick statistical sample; apparently no one that I know has had a three-day headache except me, just before I was diagnosed with a brain tumour.

It was at this point that I produced a new and updated list of things Lu needs to do on my death. I also asked Carl (a computer geek) to have a quick 'check' of my laptop. In my research for this book, I may have stumbled upon certain unsavoury images online that I would not like others to see. Best to get everything nice and tidied up, and for Carl to leave me with a nice clean reputation and hard disk.

Lu phoned the hospital and they told me to come in for a scan. The first available appointment was a day later, on Lu's birthday! I already had my hospital bag packed. Normally I have to book a scan three months in advance. This time the hospital proceeded very quickly. Nothing to worry about. The team there were obviously just trying to be helpful.

Lu and I were due to have a boozy birthday lunch in a nice Central London eatery. Instead it was bad coffee and a limp sandwich whilst seated on plastic chairs in the hospital waiting room. Another event that I had screwed up for her. Every scan feels like it will end with Earth-shattering news. Yet this one had a particularly bad feeling about it.

The preliminary result was also fast: a day or so. No Pear regrowth. He had not come back (yet). Massive relief as always. But why did I still feel so crappy? Something was not quite right in my head. I'd had this feeling before and was right.

*

A couple of days after Lu's birthday, we were both sitting down to breakfast when, suddenly, I started slurring my words. Before you judge me – no, I had not touched a drop. I could come in here with a quip about recently joining a wine club and how we meet each morning at 9.00am in the park. But no. Completely sober. Lu then told me that my face had gone all asymmetric. My face is a bit asymmetric as I have a mole on one side. However, this was properly different on each side. Like my face came from two different people (albeit both white and in their forties) who were experiencing very different emotions. Left side of face was saying:

"I'm fine, can we stop worrying and get on with breakfast."

Right was saying:

"I'm so sad that my mouth is actually drooping like a cartoon Adam after a big rock falls on his foot."

So the sides of my face were unable to decide in unison what expression to do.

Lu and I are both fairly clued up on basic first aid, and we both knew what it was. It is called a Transient Ischaemic Attack (or TIA), more commonly known as a 'mini-stroke'. The term 'mini' disguising how serious it actually is (or can be). They may as well have called it a 'fun-sized stroke'. This little cutesy name starting with 'mini' gives the ailment an aura of being a mischievous little imp at most. This is not helped by the fact that something so serious as a stroke uses the same name as the verb of what one does to a puppy.

If I ever discover a deadly serious illness I will call it:

'Cuddlebun'

to take the sting out of the diagnosis. A less serious version that does not kill instantly will be named:

'Mini-Cuddle'

The effects passed, and Lu and I decided to just keep an eye on things. I could not face another evening in A&E nor a conversation with my doctor's receptionist. So we left it.

This means that I am now a cancer victim who has had a stroke. Life just gets better and better. Should I now get two seats on the Tube? Let's run through this again: cancer and stroke. Wait – there's one missing for the full hat-trick of terrible health (and to get three seats) – I need a heart attack to complete the set. Unfortunately, my ticker is in pretty good shape. Shame really that it did not end up in somebody who was going to get better use out of it. So my list of ailments now reads:

1) Cancer.
2) Stroke (mini).
3) Fungal thing on my toe nails.

What they have in common is that they are all near impossible to fix. Number 3 is, of course, the odd one out. It does not get me a seat on a train or a wheelchair at an airport. It also does not make dinner parties go quiet when mentioned. Although, to be fair, it does tend to stop people eating.

The name for number 3 is an infestation of distal subungual onychomycosis which, ironically, possibly has the scariest name of all.

*

Life returned to my version of normality for a few days and then....it happened again. More slurring but with the added bonus of dribbling too. This time no messing and Lu, after speaking with a friend and colleague, called an ambulance immediately. An ambulance??! But I felt fine! Ambulances are for heart attacks and broken legs. Not speech impediments and drooling. I felt like a fraud, guilty of wasting taxpayers' money and medics' time & resources.

When the paramedics arrived, I told them this and asked if all these blue flashing lights and fancy kit was a bit of an overreaction. Absolutely not they tried to assure me. They had attended four call outs that afternoon and of the four, mine was the most worthy of an emergency phone call.

I still thought they were all fussing about nothing. I was on my feet, doing the clearing up. If they were worried about me, maybe I could go in by public transport? No, they were insistent this was right up there with other medical emergencies. But, I protested:

"I'm on my feet. People who need ambulances are not on their feet. They're lying on the floor at the base of a ladder or rolling around clutching their chest. Look I'm fine!"

I then gave them a reassuring smile – at least half of my face did. I thanked them for their concern and offered the paramedics a whisky. Sounded like they'd had a tough afternoon. It made me wonder what the other three call outs were about which were even less worthy of an ambulance. Possibly a dangerously dry scalp. I could imagine the paramedics radioing in from the ambulance:

[Radio static] *"Base, this is unit Alpha Four on blue light call out in Muswell Hill, North London. We have just attended to the scalp patient. Patient is on board and we can confirm that, as feared, it is indeed a severe dandruffic episode. I repeat* [more radio static] *SDE Grade One. Have the on-call consultant dermatologist on standby. My team has administered emergency Head and Shoulders."*

The ambulance crew confirmed that my slurring and dribbling was indeed a TIA. Now I think about it, the acronym TIA sounds just like an airline. I was going by ambulance and so travelling TIA Business Class. All this fuss for a couple of fun-sized strokes.

The paramedics were most helpful and patient. In this regard I am not proud of how I reacted to the situation. After all, they were just doing their job. It was not their fault they happened to be on call at the time I needed an ambulance during a particularly mischievous episode. I can only apologise to them. My conversation with the lovely lady paramedic on the way to the hospital went something along these lines:

Me: *"Is this all really necessary?"*

Paramedic: *"Yes – this is standard protocol."*

Me: *"In that case, why haven't we got the sirens on? I pay my taxes. I want sirens."*

Paramedic: *"Mr Blain, we don't need sirens."*

Me: *"But sirens are really cool, and we're now stuck in traffic. I said we should have gone by tube. It would take twenty minutes tops, and cost nothing to the tax payer."*

Me again: *"Can I sit in the front?"*

Paramedic: *"No, it would not be safe."*

Me: [whiny toddler voice] *"But he's sitting in the front. It must be my turn now. And he gets to do this every day."*

Paramedic: *"Yes, he's the driver."*

Me: *"Can I have some gas please?"*

Paramedic: *"Why? Are you in pain?"*

Me: *"Not really. I just fancied some and I can't see a drinks trolley."*

Paramedic: *"Are you going to be one of those difficult patients?"*

Me: *"I intend to be. Help me out here. What did the other 'difficult' patients get up to?"*

Paramedic: *"I feel I had better not say."*

Me: *"You don't get it. You do this every single day. For me this is exciting."*

Me again: *"Look there's a bed. Can I lie on it? I could do with a rest after all this excitement. And I've got this rubbishy sideways seat because you won't let me sit in the front. Travelling sideways like this makes me feel sick."*

[Paramedic hands me a cardboard sick bowl which looked exactly like a trilby hat and fitted me perfectly.]

Paramedic: *"So, Adam. How are you feeling?"*

Me: *"A bit sleepy. Can I lie on the bed now?"*

Paramedic: *"No, it would not be safe to lie in the bed."*

Me: *"Not safe? Why have you got it then? How can it be unsafe to travel in a bed in an ambulance? I would be lying down, in a bed, in a vehicle built like a tank, travelling at fifteen miles per hour, packed full of medicines, medical equipment and paramedics. This must be the safest place on Earth! I'll risk it."*

After a short period of stony silence, we arrived at the hospital.

Paramedic: *"Now, Mr Blain. How would you like to go into the hospital from the ambulance?"*

Me: *"I get to choose however I want?"*

Paramedic: *"Yes"*

Me: *"OK. I'll go for horseback."*

Paramedic: *"Sorry. We don't have horses."*

Me: *"Alright, I'll cycle in."*

Paramedic: *"Do you have a bicycle?"*

Me: *"No, but I don't have an ambulance either and this thing has done 99% of the journey."*

Me [pointing at a big orange canvas thing in the ambulance]. *"What's that? It looks fun."*

Paramedic: *"That's a stretcher."*

Me: *"Can I have that then? You've got one of those – I can see it."*

Paramedic: *"No you cannot go in by stretcher. Do you want a wheelchair?"*

Me: *"You said any way I choose as long as it isn't on horseback. You implied that my chosen mode of transport must be available. The stretcher is available. I checked and there's no one on it."*

Paramedic: *"Still no. It's not safe."*

Me: *"So why do you have it then?"*

Paramedic: *"It's for things like a broken leg."*

Me [whimpering]: *"So it's safe if you have a broken leg, but no use for a victim of a broken brain? That's much more serious. I want a stretcher. I've never been on one. And I've perfected my lolling."*

Paramedic: *"Please get into the wheelchair. And why are you using that sick bowl as a hat?"*

Hospital A&E

At the hospital, I had the customary six-hour wait in A&E reduced to a mere two hours. Perhaps it really was serious. Or maybe my fame and status as an F-List celebrity enabled me to jump the queue. We shall never know.

Various doctors spoke with me and conducted numerous tests including a full MRI scan of my head. They checked carefully for bleeds and other damage, but they thought it all looked OK, even if the skull was a bit empty.

The process at hospital was a bit of a blur. Lots of waiting around with Lu, sending text messages to worried friends and relations.

The end result was as good as I could hope for:

- definitely a TIA,
- no obvious and noticeable brain damage caused by it,
- no need for an operation,
- and no need to stay in hospital – go home.

I was told to keep an eye on things and

- call an ambulance immediately if there is any kind of re-occurrence,
- take aspirin regularly even without a headache. That's easy enough. We've got some of those in the bathroom.

Lu was advised to keep an eye out for any more slurring or face drooping.

This was a huge relief and off we headed back to Russell Square underground train station, ambulances no longer available to me. It was then that it struck me that, after all this commotion with ambulances, paramedics and emergency scans, the outcome was to go home and take aspirin. The exact same result as if I had pitched up complaining of a mild hangover.

Birthday

I have recently had another birthday. A period of frustration and worry for my friends and family. In my previous book, *Pear Shaped,* I explained about the difficulties of getting a birthday card for somebody's last birthday. What is even more difficult is to buy the birthday card for the subsequent years after the supposed last birthday. I had to work quite hard to create a suitable rhyme for the inside of this card but here is my best shot. It can have the first line adapted as necessary depending upon how long the person in question has been cheating death:

'It has been three years now,
Since excavating your head.
To be perfectly honest,
We thought you'd be dead.
For this special birthday, raise a glass!
You keep on living, we thought you would pass.
To survival of illness in all of its phases,
Although, we assumed, you'd be pushing up daisies'

The Quiet after the Storm

It has been a rough week. Mild headaches have returned, which become painful if I sneeze or cough. Every headache makes me worry about the reincarnation of Pear.

On top of this, the attention from all my strokes was dying down and I was running out of ideas for my writing. Then, like a knight on a white horse, in rode the NHS to my morose Sunday afternoon with a text message. Thank you, NHS! You really are the service that keeps on giving. Is there anything in your charter about assisting writers with their writer's block? Surely writer's block isn't a proper illness treatable at taxpayers' expense? Anyway, right on cue I received the following SMS in relation to my TIA emergency call:

Thinking about your A&E experience at University College London hospitals: How likely are you to recommend us to friends and family if they needed similar care or treatment?

1) *Extremely likely*
2) *Likely*
3) *Neither likely nor unlikely*
4) *Unlikely*
5) *Extremely unlikely*
6) *Don't know*

Reply today, your feedback is anonymous and important to us.

To recap, I had a stroke or possibly had had one. I was advised by two doctors (Lu and her colleague) to call an ambulance.

The paramedics agreed I was correct to do so and that such action potentially saved my life. So my response was a '1', obviously.

If you are able to text back at all, I think you should be compelled to rate the hospital (as above) as a 1 or 2. You should only be able to score them in the 4 to 6 range if your initial response to the questionnaire was:

Aaaaaaaaaah [death emoji – you know with 'x' instead of eyes]

I think the patients should get a text back from the NHS depending upon the initial response given. The hospital wants feedback. Patients need it too. That is feedback on our feedback. I am the one without a full brain. I want to check I am operating as a normal member of society. I do not wish to put the hospital to any more trouble when it has done so much for me. I want to help, so here are my suggested automatic reply texts for each chosen option, which I invite the hospital to use:

1) *Extremely likely*

NHS automated text reply:

OK You're normal.

2) *Likely*

NHS automated text reply:

So what else were you thinking of? What alternative do you have troubling you from the back of your mind that leaves you needing to hedge your bets somewhat?

3) *Neither likely, nor unlikely*

NHS automated text reply:
Congratulations! You are the first person ever to have chosen this option. Is there really anybody on the entire planet 'neither likely, nor unlikely' to recommend calling an ambulance when they see someone having a stroke? We actually did not think we needed this option. We only put it in to comply with government guidelines on showing no bias in our communications. In fact, Les from IT was going to miss this off the list, but thank goodness he didn't. Let's recap. So you recently witnessed a stroke and either you, or someone near you, quite correctly called for an ambulance on this phone number. The paramedics turned up, did their thing, helped this poor sod and took him to hospital for treatment and tests, potentially saving his life. Now, hypothetically, let's say the exact same thing happens again a week later. The soon-to-be-widow shrieks out in distress:

"Shall I call an ambulance?"

Would you react the same way or would you say:

"I know it is a stroke, I have my phone on me. But do you know what? Damn it! Let's just see how this thing plays out."

I bet you are one of those really annoying people that goes round to others for dinner and when asked, at the end of the meal:

"Tea or coffee?"

asks the host to run through all the teas in their cupboard and then says something like:

"Yes, I will have the peppermint infusion, but do you have one without the fennel extract and with rose-hips instead?"

You're a bit of a twat, aren't you? Please respond to this text with one of the following options:

1) *Yes, I'm a twat and, as such, I can't operate a phone properly.*
2) *I resent that. I'm not a twat. I just have my reasons – leave it at that. You asked the bloody question and I answered it from the list of options. If you don't like my choice, why give it to me as an option?*
3) *I neither know or don't know whether or not I'm a twat. Please repeat the question. I'm too thick to realise you don't have to repeat the question because I can just re-read the message.*

4) *Unlikely*

NHS automated text reply:

You bastard. So you wanted them to die? Wouldn't want to be your friend.

5) *Extremely unlikely*

NHS automated text reply:

Look. We know where you live, Sicko.

6) *Don't know*

NHS automated text reply:

What sort of fucking idiot does not know if he would call an ambulance after witnessing a stroke, having just gone through the whole process a few days beforehand? Now give the phone back to a grown up, you moron. We even have a choice for those evil bastards that would ***not*** *call an ambulance. So you are even harder to categorise than someone who would sit to one side and watch the stroke victim die. It's you that needs treatment, mate.*

As I said, I must be quite normal because I texted back '1'. The NHS were not satisfied with this answer and replied immediately:

Please tell us the main reason for the score you have given.

My response:
I am 'normal', at least this is what your survey indicates. Am I not in the only category that should avoid cross-examination of my response? As 'normal', I take no pleasure in watching somebody slowly die from the effects of a stroke when they are lying there and, with their dying breath, shout out:

'Quickly, I am having a stroke. Can anybody make a recommendation of somebody to call?'"

This got me thinking about what alternatives there are to calling an ambulance, as the original text message suggests there has to be one. This must involve phoning around private health care providers to see who has the best deal on. All this whilst sprawled out, slurring and dribbling.

The conversation may go:
Me: *"I need urgent health insurance that covers strokes and emergency transport to hospital."*

Insurer: *"We can provide that cover but do not provide ambulances. Only third party operated air ambulances in certain extreme circumstances, and where the insured party is abroad. Is there any particular reason you ask?"*

Me [still slurring and dribbling]: *"It was just the first ailment that came into my head. Hang on, I think my drool is shorting the phone."*

Insurer: *"We do not provide this cover for what is known as 'existing conditions'. Have you ever had a stroke before?"*

Me: *"It depends when you are asking."*

Insurer: *"I am asking you now."*

Me: *"As of an hour ago, I was virtually completely stroke-free. As a mental estimate, I would say that even now, well over ninety nine percent of my life has been entirely stroke-free."*

Insurer: *"When do you wish the cover to start?"*

Me: *"Yesterday. Or an hour ago if that's cheaper. Can we pretend I am phoning this morning? It is only just lunch time. Don't tell me you are going to wriggle out of providing me cover for the sake of about an hour. You insurers, you're all the bloody same."*

Insurer: *"It sounds to me as if you have an existing condition. If so, we cannot provide you with cover. Otherwise it would be like trying to place a bet on a horse after it has just won the race."*

Me: *"I'm not exactly sure how I've 'won'. I'm lying here having a stroke, hypothetically at least. Actually, It's not like that at all. It's like phoning the knacker's yard when the horse has collapsed at the second jump, is lying on the ground dribbling out bits of semi-digested grass and only able to say 'neigh' out of one side of its face. I'm hardly going to call the knacker's yard if my horse has just won. I'd be calling stud farms. Why would I* ***not*** *call a* *health insurer when I am worried about getting very ill? That's the basis of your business model isn't it? Anyway, I recently signed up to the AA and they let me join after I had broken down. I did not have to join, wait ten minutes and then phone them up: I have cover with you from today. As a stroke of good fortune, I have just broken down. Thank goodness I did not sign up half an hour later."*

Back to my texting. In the end, I texted back thanking them for their help. Whilst totally satisfied with my treatment, the NHS may not be the first governmental body I call next time I have a stroke. Nothing personal, and I stress I would recommend you to a friend who is dying. However, for me, next time I will call the Department of Environment. You know where you are with the good old DoE which is therefore my 'go to' government body of choice. Also, if things do not go in my favour, the disposal of my body will become an environmental issue rather than a medical one.

Emergency Scan Results

A week after my hospitalising TIA, I went back to get more detailed scan results. Unsurprisingly my anxiety took on a new level compared to the regular quarterly scans. The atmosphere of the waiting area seemed different. Were the nurses avoiding eye contact or was I just being paranoid? When the consultant called me in, all became clear.

So at this point in time, I do not have brain cancer visible on a scan. I merely have clearly detectable, permanent brain damage. Well that's a huge relief! Rather than being on the border of death, I have now advanced to taking the first couple of steps towards being a vegetable. I hope it's a potato as I like chips, crisps and mash. Nothing unpleasant like kale or too up-market like mange tout. Just a common potato.

This latest setback is caused by Pear's departure, as well as collateral damage from the surgery and radiotherapy. The TIA was actually a symptom of this damage, not a cause. This means that if the unimaginable and nearly impossible occurs and I am 'cured', I still end up mental. Life just gets better and better. I saw the scan for myself. A big hole where the clever bit of brain is meant to be (as opposed to the bit that deals with breathing, heart beating and other general body admin).

This official brain damage has a number of consequences which, looking back, were beginning to reveal themselves before this latest drama:

- I lose my keys, wallet, glasses and phone around the house and spend half of my available time looking for them;

- Whenever I walk past a care home, I always look in through the window to see which armchair I would pick. Near a window (hopefully open to get fresh air), but also with an unobstructed view of the television.
- About a year after surgery, I had my IQ measured to see how much Pear had taken. I was relieved to score 141. This is classified as 'genius or near genius'. A further eighteen months on and I now cannot find my way back from an unfamiliar toilet without texted directions sent to me, or a handler walking me back. I feel like an ex-circus strongman who has reached the stage where he needs help carrying the shopping in from the car.

Depressingly, this means that Pear is actually the clever bit of me. Nowadays, Pear is half eaten by cancer and lives in a hospital freezer. It must be frustrating for him. He has all that brain power and intelligence, but wastes his time trying to communicate with the ice cream and frozen peas.

Despite having nearly killed me, I do miss Pear and want him back. It must be cold and lonely for him with nothing to do but to try to re-assemble chopped frozen veg back into its original form like a 3D jigsaw. Having to do it without the benefit of limbs. With no mouth, he cannot even eat the ice cream.

I have thought about busting him out in a daring jail break. We could then go on the run together like *Thelma & Louise* (well, he can't run, but I would help him). We would have lots of fun adventures together and I would help with the most challenging crosswords.

I could not be arrested for theft as Pear belongs to me. Nor could I be charged with kidnapping as Pear should be part of me. Nobody could dispute either of these points. I could even prove it with a scan. Pear will be the exact size and shape of the hole left in my brain.

Having said all this, it is possible my brain damage is not cancer treatment related. You see, my favourite accident is to bang my head. I do this head-banging a lot (and hard), applying the adage that, if you are going to do something at all, then do it properly. It happens spectacularly each morning whilst un-stacking the dishwasher. I stand up with a double armful of plates and, in doing so, hit my head on the corner of the mug cupboard door. I suspect that this is causing the brain damage, rather than merely a symptom of it. The alternative is that Pear has the part of the brain that broadcasts:

"You're a bloody idiot, Blain. Look what you're about to do. You would think you would have learnt by now, having had this accident every morning."

Alternatively, Pear has the memory bit that covers what I do just before eating breakfast each morning – empty the dishwasher, bang my head in the process.

Short Term... Nope, it's Gone

The most annoying part of my brain damage is the increased memory loss. As mentioned, I constantly lose my wallet, phone and glasses. The phone is not so bad because, provided I haven't left it in 'Do Not Disturb' mode, I can ring it and follow the sound. Assuming I left it in the building I am in. Unfortunately, there is no similar function for my wallet or glasses, neither of which (to my knowledge) has its own phone number.

I have gone a long way towards 'curing' myself of this memory loss by buying a bum bag/fanny pack. I personally use the former expression because in real English it sounds less like a container for holding feminine sanitary products. Into this go the above critical items, as well as keys, pens and other odds and ends essential to my life. I clip this bum bag to myself and never let it go. At least that is the theory. I am 'cured' not in the sense of my brain being better; I have just found a way of not needing a brain. The question:

"Where have I put my phone/wallet/glasses/keys?"

has not gone away, but the answer has become a simple:

"Look down, you idiot."

The bum bag is not infallible. Problems arise from either forgetting to put stuff in it or losing the entire bumbag on the rare occasions I take it off – basically for showers and bed. My bumbag is not waterproof, which rules out showering with it. I cannot wear it in bed as the bum bag is so full that I cannot turn over – believe me, I've tried.

Another disadvantage stems from the 'all eggs in one basket' issue. I lose the bumbag and my entire life goes into a tail-spin. If I am outside, I cannot let myself in, phone for help or write a note. Nor can I access the map on my phone. I cannot even see the house without glasses, let alone get in. I become befuddled and helpless. Being a marsupial would help enormously as your pouch never goes anywhere. Furthermore, I am 47 years old. My imminent demise would no longer be a tragedy but a good, ripe old age for a kangaroo. It may also improve my boxing skills. At the time of writing this trans-species conversion is not available on the NHS.

This use of a bum bag is one way in which I deal with an incomplete and damaged brain. It is one of many examples in which the basic common-sense bit of brain (thankfully retained) can compensate for Pear's absence.

*

Another constant problem arises from my use of WhatsApp group chat. I cannot distinguish my messages from those of my buddies. The issue is that my messages are highlighted by a bright green background, signifying (to me) importance, like something someone else may say. It is not that I do not say important things, it's just that they come from my head, so I ought to know them. Hence no need for phone manufacturers to highlight them, particularly not in bright green. Last night, whilst trying to organise a lads' curry, I ended up getting into an argument with myself about the date we were meeting. It got quite heated at one point and I was accused of being difficult and inflexible. I thought the accuser himself was the one causing the problems, so I let him know in no uncertain terms. Having admonished myself, I am now not speaking with myself – at least for a few days. That will teach me.

More Medication

Both Lu and I were getting concerned about how absent-minded I was becoming. It came to a head when I started putting the TV remote controls in the fridge. After all, there was space now the screwdriver bit was gone. However, this led the family to the conclusion that I needed more medication. This time to make me less stupid.

At my next medical appointment, with me sitting there with another cardboard sick bowl on my head, the doctor took little persuading and put me on medication for preventing the progression of dementia.

Things for me have improved considerably since starting this treatment. Just the other day I scored a hat trick when I knew:

- what day of the week it was,
- where all the kids were, and
- why I had gone upstairs.

That Cambridge education is really starting to pay off! The answers were, respectively:

- Wednesday,
- downstairs fighting in front of the television, and
- I can't remember now but I knew at the time. Probably my glasses.

Unfortunately, I ran into problems last week when I finished the last of my 'clever-pills' (as I call them). I needed to order more from the Pharmacy/Doctor. Yet, having run out, I could not remember to do so. I was in a vicious circle. What the manufacturers should do is put days of the week on the blister package (as in contraception pills etc.). When the fourth from end one is popped out, it would send an automatic electronic signal to the chemist who then rings you up. Or even just a little note in with that pill. Just a thought. In the end, as with everything, Lu sorted it. After all, it's in both of our interests to prevent me from becoming too thick.

*

To me, this medication is keeping any dementia-related behaviour at bay. To other, supposedly professional mind analysers, I have developed some odd habits. So rather than the following few paragraphs being classified as Pets or Hobbies, I am categorising it as Brain Damage. You will see why.

I have an affection for snails. This is inexplicable to others but to me, makes perfect sense. They look sweet with those little stalk things sticking out and I love the way they adorably squeeze back into their shells when they get frightened or overwhelmed. In this sense they are surprisingly good communicators. Yet they have a rough time of life. They move so slowly – literally at a snail's pace. However, their only source of defence is to retreat into their shell which is actually totally inadequate. Snails round here have two main enemies: birds and shoes. Both of these can break their shell very easily. It is like us trying to make ourselves bullet-proof using only cling film and egg shell. They have not evolved enough to develop their own kevlar.

It is worse than that for snails, though. They leave a trail of wet slime which is fine if travelling on damp mud or dew-covered leaves. Not such fun on a parched pavement or road covered in dust and sand. This must slow them down further and make them completely parched. The nearest human equivalent to the bottom of a snail (in texture and wet sliminess) must be the tongue. Think how unpleasant it is when your tongue touches something hot, dry and dirty, like a train company meat pie. Now imagine everywhere you travel involves rubbing your tongue along such a surface. Suddenly popping to the shops becomes a major ordeal, as it is for a snail. You would dread your wife requesting that you lick your way to the corner shop to get some milk.

For these reasons, I rescue snails. Any snail in my path that is on a bit of dry pavement and therefore likely to be crushed by a passing brogue, gets rescued and placed in a nice damp spot in some hedge. To snails, I am their Guardian Angel. I am also their version of a Dignitas nurse. If I see one that is semi-squished and clearly going to die (a snail, not a Dignitas nurse), I put them out of their misery by stomping on them properly. Nothing too crazy with my behaviour so far, I'm sure you will agree. However, when euthanizing a snail, I also:

- say a few nice words about 'Cyril' or whatever his/her name is,
- conduct a quick prayer, and
- put together a small shrine for other gastropods to visit and pay their respects.

I hope I get my just rewards when I am in my final moments. Perhaps the Dignitas nurses will quickly stomp on me to give a speedy and pain-free death, before I am eaten by a pigeon.

My affection does not extend to slugs, even though they are pretty similar, plus or minus a shell. I cannot explain this. Snails are cute and lovely; slugs are slimy and horrible. Examining this, it probably gives some indication of the roots of racism. Anyway, I am a snailist and I hold my head high.

This all sounds perfectly rational, does it not? So why do others see this as a symptom of brain damage?

It all started when I saw a snail in my path with a hole in its shell. I have no expertise in snails but assumed the shell does not heal up. There is a section of our front garden which is dark, damp from a dripping overflow pipe and has lots of leaves to eat and provide cover from birds. This became my recently opened snail hospital. No waiting lists, no over-crowded wards, no paper work. We'll just pop you in here and see if that shell of yours heals up. It didn't, but I was very much learning on the job.

Admittedly, it is a pretty basic hospital. The nurses are other snails who are 'graduates' from my hospital, distinguished by the cross I draw in Tippex on their shells. They do need some form of uniform to distinguish them from patients.

The snail hospital is not without problems:

- The Intensive Care Unit becomes the morgue/crow cafeteria, on an almost weekly basis.
- There is a constant lack of snail medication and the nurses keep deserting their posts. They should learn from our

> wonderful NHS nurses. I have never heard of a hospital nurse, in the middle of their shift, running off because they see a clump of rotting moss on a neighbour's wall.

I am sure my hospital would fail any Care Quality Commission inspection. On the plus side, though, there are no waiting lists. Or any lists at all for that matter.

The snails usually leave, either on their own or in the stomach of a crow, but it gives them a chance and I am doing my bit for snail-kind.

For some reason this altruistic gesture of kindness to a fellow-species is taken by my psychologists as further evidence of my dysfunctional brain. I will leave you, my readers, to decide on the validity of this assessment.

Dying to Relax

I go for long walks in the evening. A chance to pound out some stress, get a bit of exercise and listen to loud music. As I escape into my own world for an hour or two, the ghastly nature of real life fades into the background. I have to do this to stay sane, or to try to achieve sanity (depending upon the day).

I cannot do real exercise such as running or football because it totally exhausts me. In the latter case, I cannot play well enough to not be humiliated in public. So I walk and walk and walk, pacing the streets of East Finchley and Muswell Hill.

I download music from my on-line streaming service. Generally upbeat stuff with a good slant towards seventies and eighties rock. In fact, Spotify has got the hang of my tastes and has taken it upon itself to recommend a special playlist just for me based upon my perceived preferences. This playlist is named (by them) as

Air Punch

I have mixed emotions about this. On the one hand, I do not like being judged and summarised in two words by an algorithm. I have two words to summarise the creators of this service, but I cannot share them just in case my parents-in-law are reading this. A politer way of putting it would be – presumptuous.

On the other hand, my categorisation could have been a whole lot worse than 'Air Punch'. With my seventies ballads and plenty of calming music too, I could have been categorised as *Cardigan* or *Bifocals.*

Whilst walking, I drift into part meditation, part fantasy. Why not live for an hour in a fantasy world? The real one has turned out pretty awful. This pacing of my frustrations into submission is a few hours of 'me time'. Away from daily stresses. Away from my arch-nemesis Cancer, and his side-kick Brain Damage.

In my fantasy world I have super powers (proper super powers, not the rubbish ones I actually have). I fight violent criminals whilst also being leader of this country. I am, of course, the best prime minister ever and a well-loved super hero. It is a difficult balance though. You do not want to go too far with the fantasy as it loses any realism. There must be elements of the mundane to make the experience more realistic and plausible. One must not over-egg the pudding. Hang on!! Why must I not over-egg the pudding? It is a fantasy so real rules don't apply. I can over-egg it as much as I want. In fact, I can make it one hundred percent egg. What's the point of having a fantasy world where I spend my time filing away the old electricity bills and then sorting out the recycling? If I am going to be the best and most popular leader the UK has ever had, why then fantasise myself into a coalition government or hung Parliament? I do not go into details about manifestos and policies other than a ban on embroidered pillow cases.

Anyway, as I mentioned above, you do not want to ditch ALL plausibility otherwise the fantasy loses its bite of realism. To give the authentic touch to my super-hero, and as a nod to reality, he has haemorrhoids. How could there be a made-up superhero with piles? So it's real!

Now please excuse me because I need to get back to over-powering those terrorists holding disabled orphans as hostages. The only weapon available to me is an egg whisk I picked up from the orphanage kitchen. Don't worry, I prevail and the terrorists are all lightly aerated to death.

*

It rained heavily yesterday. Eventually it slowed to spitting and this was my opportunity. So I put on my waterproof shoes and warmest jacket and headed out to punch some air (being one of the few things that I am allowed to punch under English law).

Now I do not generally have a problem with bus drivers. However, the ones in my area seem to be unusually unpleasant for no particular reason. There is the usual stuff, such as when you run the distance of three bus stops to catch up with the bus and the driver waits until your nose is pressed against the closed door before setting off without you.

If I do make it onto the bus, I realise that I am not the only victim of bus drivers' attitude. I hear them say things like:

"*You can't bring that wheelchair on the bus. We already have a buggy and that is our full allowance of bus-borne vehicles.*" or "*You can't bring that buggy on the bus. It's far too.... pink*".

Yesterday, many of the roads contained giant puddles – almost lakes. These are a nightmare for pedestrians. On the road I was pounding down, the pavements are narrow and there was a giant puddle taking up much of the road. A bus was speeding towards me and I had nowhere to go to escape the drenching. My only option was to step on to a nearby zebra crossing thus requiring the bus to stop. I wanted to cross the road anyway. So I stepped out on to the semi-submerged zebra crossing, pleased that I had found a way through this. Strangely, the approaching bus was not slowing down. In fact, it seemed to speed up. The bus kept going and I was forced to dive on to the pavement, chased by a tsunami of rain water which found and engulfed me. Not only did the driver not apologise, he seemed offended and played the victim when I flipped him the bird and used some choice words from my swearcabulary.

In his defence, the driver would question how he could possibly have known there was a zebra crossing there (what with it being underwater) with the only clues being:

- a sign on the road warning of a zebra crossing;
- two massive, flashing beacons either side of the road;
- a pedestrian standing between the two flashing zebra crossing beacons glaring straight back at the driver in an uncompromising and self-righteous manner;
- the fact that the driver might have only ever driven along this particular stretch of road (in both directions) a mere seven or eight times a day (four only on a Sunday) over the last few years.

Dogging All Day Long

By now you will know that I have always wanted a dog. I had considered this to be another project I would take on in retirement. Well now I am in retirement and still (just) on my feet. I am also running out of time, particularly with a pet that can live fifteen years. I may not even make it to the dog's third birthday – and that's in dog years.

Back to one of the basic principles I apply to life these days: *"If you're going to do something significant, do it now and don't wait."*

However, the downside with such a pet is that it's very likely to outlive me. This longevity point is an issue with many possible pets. If I want a pet I am confident of outliving, perhaps I should only consider mayflies. Owning a dog does not work without me around to walk it because most days, Lu is at work and the kids are at school. This is why having a dog has been off limits.

Despite it being such a stupid, impractical and risky idea, Lu knew how much it would mean to me. So she spent hour upon hour every day searching dog rescue websites for suitable adoptees. Each evening, she would fall in love with a different canine.

It was reaching the stage where Lu's dog-surfing activities were becoming an obsession, taking up valuable hours of every evening. For us, the tipping point came when I calculated that, even taking into account the many walks and trips to the vets that a dog would require, she would have more time on her hands owning a dog rather than shopping for one.

The moment arrived when we could resist no longer, despite the fact that we knew full well it was a stupid decision. Extra stupid on the basis that we knew it was stupid at the time we made it. So we went to a dog rescue centre out in the middle of Essex. Just to look. Yeh right! What was amazing was that we only came back with one dog rather than a whole car load.

So welcome to the family gorgeous, food-obsessed Lola! She eats anything and everything whether or not that thing could be classified as 'food' for dog or human. If the thing is not edible to either species, she will either eat it anyway or chew it to pieces. We do not know her exact breed, but our best guess is part Labrador and part commercial Wood Chipper. She fitted straight into our family and has dramatically improved our lives. As far as really stupid decisions go, this is the best we have ever made.

*

I spend hours and hours with Lola as she now joins me on my epic pacing of North London as well as the school run (on foot). My favourite thing in life now is to walk with my new companion. Much better than walking with a human. I have somebody to talk to, listen to me and yet I do not have to deal with their crap. Alright, a bad choice of words, because I do have to wrap it up in a little bag. But I do not have to listen to her problems (unless it is kennel cough).

I never realised this before but there is a whole parallel universe of dog owners. A society that constantly greets and chats to each other. Total strangers chin-wagging on the street, provided that the topic of conversation is initially dog-related. Young, attractive mums come up to me all the time to pet Lola. It is like I have suddenly become very attractive (although the attractive part of me is on a lead at the end of my arm). Why didn't I think of this when I was single?

*

One of the most important dog ownership lessons I have learnt is that, however well trained you think your dog is, they can always surprise you. Lola is not at all well trained. When asked what tricks she can do, and what skills she possesses, I can only boast two:

- The majority of her 'doings' are not in the house. Well over 70%.
- Lola does not bite anyone ever, other than me, on my ears, when I play with her.

Last week, we took Lola to a close family member's house. My fabulous cousin, Oliver, is a qualified Rabbi. He invited all of us round for lunch and he was dog-sitting his sister's female dog – I cannot bring myself to use the 'B word'. Saying, for example:

"Can I bring round my new bitch, Lola?"

makes me sound like a pimp looking for business.

The two dogs hit it off immediately; too well in fact. After the initial butt-sniffing greeting, relations evolved into an hour-long display of full-on doggy lesbianism whilst we ate lunch (or tried to). I am not in any way homophobic. I am just saying that I would be singularly unimpressed if two of my gay friends got it on big time with an X-rated display of affection during lunch at a Rabbi's house. Now I think about it, let's extend this to straight friends too. And acquaintances. And to the abode of any religious minister during any meal time. And in respect of any animal. So, two squirrels (of either gender, same or different) openly exploring their sexuality at a pagan priest's house, during elevenses would also be unacceptable. There is no prejudice based upon sexuality, religion, gender or species. It just boils down to that ancient adage:

"Get a room!"

Which should really be qualified to:

"Get a room in which nobody is eating!"

Lesotho

One thing that has survived the barrage of cancer, radiotherapy, stroke and brain damage is my long-term memory. I can still reminisce about my pre-cancer life. I have had many great experiences and I am grateful for them and the memories they have left.

Straight after university, I spent a year as a teacher of maths and science in a remote African school in the mountain kingdom of Lesotho. Very remote indeed. My only means of communication was post. The nearest telephone was a six-hour drive away. It was the pre-internet era.

Lesotho was a dangerous place back then and I was quite vulnerable as an isolated expat. Partly for company, and partly for protection, I adopted some local dogs. Not formally adopted. There was no paperwork involved. These dogs roamed the area and were semi-domesticated, which meant they were also semi-wild. They slept outside in temperatures of -20°C and were therefore, pretty tough animals. They were not fed but survived by scavenging. Whenever I left my mountain for the bright lights of the capital, Maseru, I bought a big bag of dog biscuits to supplement their paltry diet. By feeding them, they included me and my shack as part of their territory and so protected me. We just kind of adopted each other.

One of my dogs was called *Mum-dog.* She had given birth to most of the dogs in the area (hence the name) and had a physique demonstrating this. She was fierce. In fact, she had a reputation in town as being the fiercest dog in the area. No one would come near my house because of her.

One night, I awoke to the sound of someone on the roof above me, trying to break into my shack. Then, along came Mum-dog doing her nightly rounds. From the comfort of my bed I listened to banging followed by growling, snarling, barking, tearing and quite a few swear words in local dialect. Then screaming and running. Mum-dog was awarded an extra-large breakfast for her night-shift work.

Mum-dog sometimes followed me into class which made the pupils behave extra well. This was not the strangest thing to happen to me in an African classroom, though. I also visited my brother when he was doing Voluntary Service Overseas at a school in Eritrea and helped him with taking a maths class. The oddest thing about this lesson was not that a donkey followed me into the classroom and proceeded to follow me around like a deluded stalker, convinced he could not be seen. The weirdest thing was that not one single pupil batted an eyelid. When I was at school, as part of a group of pupils, we got a bigger reaction if a wasp flew into the classroom – the entire class went into a total panic.

Back to Mum-dog. To me, the loveliest and most loyal dog. Her only downside was that she was racist. Not like a grand-parent making slightly inappropriate comments which are kind of racist (she was a dog, after all). Instead, properly full on racist. She was kind and licky to me, my western buddies and visitors. Yet she barked and growled at any pupils coming near my house. I am not qualified to go into dog psychology. I don't think this is some deep-rooted white supremacist philosophy (she was white in colour). It was just that the only people that gave her food and petted her were the other westerners and me. The only people to throw rocks at her were locals.

Life was pretty hard for a dog in Lesotho. One day, she stumbled into my house having, it transpired, consumed poison left for one of the other school dogs (who had been troubling sheep in the area). We tried to nurse her, but without any medicines whatsoever and no veterinary knowledge, it was a hopeless case. What was most tragic and moving about all this was the manner in which she died. She was more of a wild dog than a domestic one and, as such, refused to die inside my house. With her last ounce of strength, she dragged herself out of the door and died on the doorstep. In my arms. Collateral damage in the botched murder of one of the other dogs.

Why am I recalling all this? It kind of represents a mark which I have nearly reached, or feel like I am reaching. With all this cancer, numerous strokes and radiation-caused brain damage, I do sometimes feel at the stage where I need to crawl outside and die. My time has come.

More Psychologists

Following my diagnosis of brain damage, I am seeing more psychologists to assess the level and monitor the progress of my dementedness.

I went for one such session this week to check how able I was at estimating things. This apparently shows how well my brain is working/not working. It is not so much the answer that they are looking for, but the pattern of logic applied to get to an answer. First question from the psychologist:

"How far is it from London to Paris?"

This begs various questions including: What part of London? What part of Paris? What route? No assistance given in relation to these points. So I assumed it would be Charing Cross to the Eiffel Tower, measured as the crow flies. I said 230 miles. Not bad at all. It was comfortably within the un-moronic range. The psychologist just wanted to ensure I did not say 'Eleven foot' or 'Three billion light years'. The answer is 214 miles, so I was accurate to within ten percent. So far, so comfortably sane. Next question:

"How many camels are there in London?"

Again, I immediately ruled out what I considered to be ridiculous. More than one, or else London Zoo would have a pretty sparse Large Desert Mammal section. However, I don't own one and nor, to my knowledge, do any of my neighbours. I cannot remember seeing one tethered up outside a supermarket whilst I was petting other people's dogs. Therefore, it would also be clearly wrong to say:

"Millions and millions – in fact, since the epidemic, they now outnumber people."

I estimated eight. Good enough and I was certified

"Not a total idiot."

All was going well until the journey home when, out of curiosity, I checked the answer to the camel question on my phone. No specific answer but, on the edge of London, there is a camel park. What the hell! I did not even know there was such a thing as a 'camel park'. Its very presence makes me likely to fail the test as my answer could be out by a factor of ten. I am not even sure that I know what a camel park is. A series of slides and roundabouts, designed for and used by camels? A place to park your camel whilst in the shops? Do remember to pay for and display your ticket where it can clearly be seen, such as glued to the tethered camel's forehead.

Neither of these apparently. The term 'camel zoo' or 'camel farm' would be a whole lot less confusing.

I then had to phone the psychologist to confess about this park so that he could adjust his figures for me. I, of course, also rang the camel park to complain:

Me: *"Is that the camel park?"*

Camel Park Lady: *"Yes, sir. It is."*

Me: *"Have you got more than one or two camels?"*

Camel Park Lady: *"Yes, we have around forty"*

Me: *"You bastards!"*

Camel Park Lady: *"Excuse me? Are you from an animal liberation group?"*

Me: *"No. Are you planning to cull any in the near future?"*

Camel Park Lady: *"No."*

Me: *"You absolute bastards. It is because of you that I have lost my mental capacity for estimation." [Starting to get even more angry] "I am disabled and this has made me more disabled. That makes you racists."*

When my rant died down a little:

Camel Park Lady: *"Perhaps you could come and visit the park some time?"*

Me muttering: *"Yeh – with a crossbow. Then I'd be right."*

Camel Park Lady: *"Sir, I am hanging up now and calling the police."*

How disability unfriendly is it possible for an organisation to be? They had my mental health in their hands and they blew it.

Me: *"One last thing. What is your address?"*

She responded with it.

Me again: *"Yes!!! That's not a London postcode. Thank you, thank you, thank you! I love you and your camels."*

Camel Park Lady: *"I'm still calling the police."*

I am over this now and peace to all camel-kind has descended upon me. In fact, I have a soft spot for camels and a real respect for them. I have travelled a fair amount, often in countries with deserts. Therefore, I have seen and ridden quite a few camels. I love the fact that they so openly resent their domestication. In this respect, they are the total opposite of dogs. Dogs jump up, lick and wag their tails at humans (well, some dogs for some humans, but it is fairly standard behaviour). However, if you go up to domesticated camels, it is a different story. Firstly, they look down on you (both literally and figuratively) with their perpetual expression of condescension from under their huge camel eyelashes. Then they will do this raspberry blowing thing at you with their massive camel lips before spitting in your face. If you could read a dog's mind it would be thinking:

"Yeh, yeh humans. How exciting! I love you so much that I want to lick you even though you're sweaty. Now can I have some of that food?"

For camels it is even clearer:

"What is it you don't get, you dumb human? I hate you and want to go back to my desert. Can't you tell by the fact I spit in your face? Put down that sharp stick you keep poking me with and let's see how long it takes me to kick you to death with these massive hooves."

Living Will

In *Pear Shaped*, I discussed the distribution of my assets as part of my will. Read it – it's really good! A new complication has arisen, with my mini-stroke and brain damage requiring more paperwork.

Given that I may only be one stroke away from becoming a vegetable, it seemed only sensible to look into having a living will. For those of you blessedly ignorant of these documents, you write a living will whilst you are (relatively) coherent. In it, you specify the level of medical care you want to receive when you are no longer *compos mentis*, as you won't be mentally competent to do so at the time. You can request that treatment is stopped to end the torment. Alternatively, you can ask to be run into the ground and to keep going so long as a mere whiff of anything resembling life continues. I take the former approach.

This is a fun subject to discuss with your family. A real barrel of laughs. Basically how ill do I have to get before they make the decision to switch off my various life support machines to let me die? My family are not allowed to actually kill me, as that would be murder. Instead, the medics stop administering medicines and food thus ending my life by omission. So rather than a humane death, such as being shot in the head (perversely banned under English law), they let me die a slow and lingering death of starvation and submission to illness.

On the plus side, I have requested (and I am told I will get) loads and loads of drugs. For my foreign readers, I would like to point out that narcotics are generally forbidden in the UK. However, a whole different set of rules apply if you have cancer or any other terminal ailment. Drugs are banned predominantly for health reasons. Yet, if I am on my last legs, in pain or distress and about to die, then at taxpayers' expense and injected by qualified medics, there is a whole menu of various highs available to me legitimately. One ends up with quite perverse results. If, in my palliative care ward, I were to roll myself a joint and nip out to the ambulance bay for a smoke, I could be arrested. Stay where I am in my hospital bed and say that I am in distress, then some attractive, olive-skinned lady nurse will come and inject me with a hard-core opiate-based high. Basically, pure heroin. It is like saying you can have a pint of Carlsberg Special Brew containing an absinthe depth charge, yet not a cup of milky tea. I will be lying there, on my way out, hardly able to move, unable to eat and probably incontinent. Yet it's party time!! I am starting to look forward to it. Let's hope that I will be coherent enough to enjoy the experience of losing my mind to these drugs.

*

A living will includes other important information too. Let us start with the easy bit:

End of Life Care

Where would you like to be in your final days?

1) Hospital
2) Hospice
3) Home
4) High Intensity Care Unit

It's quite a choice. Although it seems that I have to pick a place starting with H. I would like to be on a ward, in a nice hospital, being cared for by scantily clad nurses in stockings, running round me like in a Benny Hill sketch. Every time a nurse trips over a mop revealing, in full, her fish-net stockings and suspender belt, a swanee whistle sound goes off. Decision made.

How do you want your body disposed of?

1) Burial
2) Cremation

The bottom line is that, by this stage, I do not really care. The way I see it is: Not My Problem. I assume that, at the time, I will have no strong opinions either way. So why not go for the cheapest option to save my family money? No horse-drawn, glass-panelled hearses for me. Modesty is the name of the game here. I would be perfectly happy with a shroud of bubble wrap, and then taken by Ford Transit to be fly-tipped in a local lay-by. There is this guy round the corner who would do it for forty quid, no questions asked. And then, of course, the celebration of my life at the mobile trailer cafe.

What type of eulogy would you like?

It would be nice to have some kind words spoken, but I would prefer those kind words to be said to me before I die so I can enjoy them. How can I verify the sincerity of my mourners if I am not alive to check? Therefore, I would like my funeral and wake to occur before I die. After all you wouldn't host a party and not pitch up yourself (alive).

So, in essence, brain damaged me today (i.e. Quite Stupid Me) has to decide for future very dysfunctional me (i.e. Very Stupid Me) when to call it a day. Quite Stupid Me literally has the power of life and death over Very Stupid Me. I do not want to sound vindictive, but I have no great affection for Very Stupid Me. In fact, I hate him and want to kill him for being such a dumb-ass. I also want Pear killed. Incinerated or turned into dog food or meat pies. Why should Pear outlive me when he is the one that caused this mess in the first place? No wait! Pear will be the only piece of me left and the only thing made up of 100% my genetics (apart from the hair in the shower).

Maybe Pear should be moved from the hospital freezer to a care home. He, in a glass jar, could be displayed to freak out the other residents. A drape could be placed over him if he misbehaves too much, like a parrot that has learnt too many swear words. Maybe the residents will become endeared to Pear as they get used to him, cooing over him and dropping the odd mint into his jar. After all, he would constantly be there to chat to; not like those grandchildren who appear, under sufferance, just once a month.

Perhaps Pear is perfectly fine, just a little bit cancery. Maybe he just needs to meet a lovely Mrs Pear, so they can run off together and skip through the meadows followed by a little herd of baby pears.

In summary then, I have requested that if I lose my marbles I am to be 'ended'. Yes, IF. Despite the above, I haven't lost it yet, apparently. The doctors have confirmed that Quite Stupid Me is still in the driving seat. If I haven't lost mental capacity at the time, then I get to decide whether or not to pull the plug. A large part of this decision will depend upon what drugs the nurses have available that week on the cocktail menu.

Commitment Issues

One thing about all of this has been particularly playing on my mind. You know those people who used to request a bell be placed in their coffin in-case they were accidentally buried alive? Well what if I am judged mentally incapacitated when I am still ok then carted off to a home long before my living will intervenes? This is my worst nightmare.

To mitigate this risk, I have come up with a series of tests I should be given to determine whether I am of sound mind or ready to be ended. It starts very subtly indeed, then gets more fundamental:

1) The inability to identify objects and distinguish one basic item from another e.g. a leaflet from a pamphlet.

A tricky one to kick off with and I would not like to be assessed on my response to this alone. As a note to Very Stupid Me: There is no cut and dried answer to this, but one sheet alone is a leaflet (even if folded). The presence of a staple or two, whilst not definitive, steers me towards it being a pamphlet. Remember this with the mnemonic: 'p' of pamphlet and the 'p' of staple. Another: 'l' for 'lone' (as in lone piece of paper) is a leaflet. I have also come up with this handy little rhyme:

A single sheet, whether folded or not,

Then it's a leaflet you will find you have got.

More than one sheet, with a staple or two;

Then it's probably a pamphlet targeted at you.

I will never remember this ode.

2) The inability to recognise close friends and relatives.

This is unless I do not want to see the person in question. In this case, pretending to be asleep is fine and does not get me carted off to a home. I do this all the time.

3) I start wearing socks with sandals.

Note: socks with slippers are fine – unless I am going for a date or a job interview. Socks with sandals – never. When I lose my dignity to this extent, it is time to quit. I would not want my children to see me like that.

4) In a queue for a supermarket checkout, I only get out my means of payment when I have reached the front of the queue. Same principle for buses and the production of bus pass.

This test should be applied universally, not just to me.

5) The inability to deal with my own 'toileting'.

I am sure that there are many happy and healthy people out their suffering from varying degrees of incontinence. However, this is not a job I could inflict upon any carer. Would they stand nearby, watching me sitting there whilst I bang out my third crossword puzzle? Would they help me with my crossword when I get stuck? Note to carers: please bring your own pen. I don't want you touching mine given the state your hands are going to be in.

I hope these rigorous tests work because I am so scared of having to go into a home or otherwise becoming institutionalised before my living will decides my fate. The state funded homes look terrible. The private homes would cost my family a fortune (which they cannot afford) and they look terrible too. Although they do have nicer cushions.

If I did end up in a care home, I would be an absolute nightmare for the staff to deal with. From the very first day, I would be planning my escape. Tunnelling through walls seems very dramatic and exciting but with my sense of direction, the tunnel would lead directly into the exercise yard or into the solitary confinement wing.

I have a plan that is easier to carry out, although it would need an accomplice from the outside world. My accomplice would smuggle me in the following items in a bag clearly marked *'Laundry – Severely Soiled. For Incineration Only'*

- a cardigan (it might get chilly);
- a flask of tea (for obvious reasons. I am going to need a cuppa after all this excitement). And finally;
- ID papers to get out and manage in the outside world. My library card will be stuck to the fridge with a magnet.

I would then make a dash for it using a laundry trolley as my escape vehicle.

Reminiscing

Yesterday, my nearest and dearest sat down together and we watched old family videos. In my position, I find this both heart-warming and poignant. After all, this is how I am going to be remembered. It will therefore form the basis of my kids' memory of me. Although the videos are only about ten years old, I look so young… and healthy. If only I had known then what was going to occur, I would have done more with the last ten years. Although I would also have had an extra decade of worrying. What is also slightly shaming (but will be of no surprise to my friends) is what I was wearing in the video. The stained T-shirt from ten years ago, that was out of shape and had multiple holes at the time, I was actually wearing whilst watching the videos.

My children looked particularly lovely, mainly because we stopped filming if a tantrum or argument arose. In particular, Sacha was so cute and chubby as a baby. He had great rolls of fat, particularly on his arms. I remember well that, during bath times, it was my responsibility to remove all the sweaty, grubby build-up of grime (sweat, skin, dirt, fluff, food etc.) that would naturally accumulate in the fat folds of his arm. In the absence of a medical word for this build-up of fermenting yuck, I referred to it as 'wrist cheese'. This distinguished it from the equivalent gunk in the folds of fat on his neck ('neck cheese' – obviously) but which was 90% food, ignoring bacteria.

This reminded me about my boys' favourite toys as toddlers. Every child has a selected cuddly toy (or several) that they love more than the others. Even when they turn to a grey/

brown colour and are more dirt than toy. For my eldest son, Jonah, it was a polar bear (imaginatively named Polar Bear) which became indispensable. We kept nearly losing him (Polar Bear that is) and spent several years looking for an identical duplicate so that we had a backup. However, it had been a gift and we never tracked one down. We therefore had to take every precaution to ensure that Polar Bear never got lost. Not easy as he came with us everywhere. Not losing Polar Bear was particularly important because Jonah would not go to sleep without him. In fact, he rarely went to sleep even with Polar Bear. After two years without rest for Lu and me, you would not think this much of a threat, but it was. We clung on, for dear life, to the two-and-a-half hours we did get. Without Polar Bear we may as well have just sold our bed and lived a sleep-free existence, eating coffee beans with a spoon, straight out of the jar. Assuming we were not going to move on to class A drugs.

For our second child, Sacha, we had learned our lesson and learnt it well. We ensured that the comfort toy he became attached to was as generic as possible. So as soon as we weaned him off the dog-shaped pencil case called Poppy (which was quite cuddly), we got him a Piglet. Not just any toy piglet. The Piglet (hence the capital 'P') as in Pooh and Piglet. Easy enough to replace at most toy shops. However, we were not fully satisfied with this. What if there was a global Piglet shortage because of some copyright dispute? We therefore got him a tea towel. Not a limited edition one like those that appear just before a Royal Wedding. A totally humdrum tea towel for drying dishes, with a blue squared pattern. You can get them anywhere and we started off with three.

We did not stop there. Each tea towel got cut up into about six smaller tea towels, each still called Tea Towel. In this regard, Tea Towels are like starfish in that each piece of Tea Towel becomes Tea Towel. A totally automatic process with no legalities or paperwork involved. We therefore started with eighteen mini Tea Towels, all indistinguishable unless you looked carefully for the stains. However, this was not as successful as we would have hoped because Sacha became attached to Piglet-Tea Towel as a combined double act. Piglet would wrap himself up in Tea Towel (if the piece was big enough) and wear it like a cape. A sort of bizarre super hero with a low budget costume. His superpower was to be able to absorb huge quantities of body secretions and food.

I thought this Piglet-Tea Towel obsession would evolve into making Sacha an ace at drying up. Sadly this did not occur. Instead, a strange coincidence happened shortly afterwards in a shirt shop. I was there with my family and the shop had a great offer available if you bought five shirts (all 100% cotton, double-cuffed and with cut-away collars – tasteful shirts). As I had to pick five, and because I had dragged my family around a shirt shop, I allowed each member of the family to pick one for me (provided it was the right size). Sacha managed to find a shirt with a blue and white squared pattern identical to Tea Towel's. Good to my word I bought and wore this shirt. On the occasions that Piglet and I were seen together, we would appear to have virtually identical outfits. People asked if Piglet and I shopped together or if my shirt came with a Piglet cape as an accessory.

Sacha's Bar Mitzvah

My youngest son, Sacha, is coming up to thirteen and, once again, we are approaching a family bar mitzvah. Lu and I decided to book things as late as possible on the basis that hosting an event is significantly more difficult if you are dead.

There is a particular part of a bar mitzvah that some of you may not be familiar with. It happens at the party afterwards, during the speeches. There is always a mention of the grandparents of the bar mitzvah boy and how lovely it is to see them there (if they are). Then there is a round of applause for the grandparents.

My mother has specifically insisted we do not do this for her, and I kind of get her point. The applause is really to congratulate them for not dying since the last family event:

"Well done for not being dead!"

is the essence of it. It begs the question, will I start getting a round of applause? If I get one, I will find it a little morbid and a reminder of what lies ahead, possibly imminently. Without it though, I would feel:

"So, you are pleased my parents are alive, but not me?"

The guests cannot win. A bit like being asked if you have stopped beating your wife – there isn't a yes/no answer that gets you out of trouble. The concept of this morbid round of applause becomes even more macabre if taken to its logical conclusion. If the elderly person in question has died in, say, the last year then surely, if mentioned in the speech, they should get booed:

"You couldn't be bothered to stay alive even for your grandson's big event."

Superpowers Update

You may be familiar with my three superpowers from the first book. How have these been affected by brain damage? Unsurprisingly, as my memory gets worse, I accept that I have now lost the power to remember all meals eaten at any restaurant in my past. My dinner party spectacular of announcing (say) that, in August 2003, I had a duck quinoa salad at a cafe in Brighton will no longer leave my fellow guests spellbound. Instead, I will need to mesmerise people by informing them of other great skills I have retained. I might point out that I remembered my keys and managed to put my trousers on correctly at my very first attempt that morning.

The power of super-smell seems to be mostly intact. To be clear for those unfamiliar with my works, it is 'smell' in the sense of being a verb. I do not have a particularly powerful odour. I can still detect certain aromas at quite an incredible distance, depending upon wind direction, even out-sniffing Lola on occasion. You would think that I should be delighted to retain this special gift, but no. It has become more of a hindrance than a benefit, and the advantages are few and far between in my life. The only real up side to this superpower is the ability to tell if a heap of clothes on my children's bedroom floor is clean or dirty without having to touch it. This is helped by the fact that my sons have now both reached puberty and so assist me by having entered their stinky phase. Even though I now do most of the household washing, I regret having this ability. In particular, there is the problem I experience with other people's body odour in restaurants. It is bearable if you just catch a whiff from a passing person on the street; but no laughing matter in a restaurant where you have to endure it for an hour or so. Whilst eating.

However, I did find a use for this superpower yesterday. I say 'use' in the loosest possible sense. I bumped into a friendly neighbour on our street. She was wearing perfume. To test my memory, I wanted to try to remember what house they lived at. I couldn't. Yet the jet stream of perfume meant I could locate the house exactly. A victory for this superpower, albeit at the expense of memory. If they had let me into their house blindfolded (you will need to come up with your own explanation as to how events could unfold this way), I could even have located which room she was in last.

Finally, the jury is still out in relation to being undetectable to bats. Worryingly, years have passed since I was last involved in a collision with a flying mammal. I have many nightmares of constantly being dive-bombed by bats that are able to divert at the last moment with me being fully detectable to them by sonar or other means. Gone are the days when I could spend many happy hours creeping up on bats before scaring them with the noise a bat predator makes.

You can see that I am a mere shell of the man I once was. My only skill left is an acute sense of smell. So, upon my death, I can be replaced by our dog.

Things I have Learnt about Cancer

Having now miraculously survived three years with this cancer, I have learnt a lot. In fact, other cancer suffers come to me for advice on how I have done this. I would love to have some real insight for them other than:

Try to be lucky

However, there are some words of wisdom I can pass on:

1) It is possible to ring-fence periods of time when you can safely put cancer away in its box and carry on with life almost as normal. Not long periods, but you can get half an hour or so. A couple of hours with practice.
2) You may have cancer (hopefully not). Remember that cancer does not have you. You are not owned by this disease.
3) Cancer does not take away your life. It just shortens it (or can do). Again, cancer does not own you.
4) Tired of taking endless pills and glugging them down with water or other liquid? You can take pills with jelly. Any flavour you like! It knocks down the pills a treat. Remember this and twice a day, instead of the chore of munching your way through a pile of pills, you are taken back to the parties of your childhood.
5) You can take pills with a spoonful of custard.
6) By the powers of extrapolation, you should be able to take pills with trifle.
7) Get a dog or rats. Or both. At least this way, you are guaranteed somebody will miss you when you die. It does not work so well with pet fish (or wasps).

Now What?

We are heading into the Winter of 2017. Fewer than ten percent with my diagnosis get to where I am today. Yet my oncologist's warning is still constantly in my mind:

"It will get you in the end."

I have never encountered anything so indiscriminate as cancer. It takes so many and has no boundaries based on gender, race, religion, ideology or age. I have lost some very dear people quite recently. People very, very loved by me and also younger than me. I will mention my wonderful, spiritual cousin Betsy, who lost her battle. You remain an inspiration to me Bets.

My fabulous friend Catherine – you were caring and never put a foot wrong in your entire, but tragically shortened, life. I have never met anyone as thoughtful and compassionate as you.

I will miss you both forever.

I do not pretend there is a happy ending for me, such as growing old with Lu in a cottage by the sea, with lots of grandchildren running around.

So I feel a mixture of emotions. Elation, for living this long and achieving quite a lot in my three years of borrowed time. But also, that my luck is not going to last much longer.

When first diagnosed, life was terrifying yet fairly straightforward. Time's up! Now get your affairs in order and wait. However tragic, at least a nice neat certainty.

Now my views on my own longevity are all over the place. Straight after a 'lovely' scan I feel overwhelmed with confidence about life. This wears off after about three weeks and changes to background concern. After two months it turns to worry. Then my stress level builds up to Results Day, when it peaks. And the cycle continues.

Yet a new emotion has appeared after the last couple of results. One that had become unfamiliar to me. I think normal people call it 'hope'. It certainly has elements of hope in there somewhere, yet it is constantly being knocked into the background by the certainty that GBM will prevail.

I do not let this new hope thing get too cocky. I maintain a document on my laptop. It is entitled:

Things for Lu to Know when I'm Dead

Not confessions. Just little things around the house I know about and she doesn't. Such as how to fix the flusher in the upstairs toilet and how to access (and stop) my subscription for razor blades.

My outlook on life can be summarised as:

Enjoy each day as it happens, but do not plan too far ahead.

'*Too far*' changes its meaning depending upon my mood, how I am feeling physically and where I am in my quarterly scan cycle. The range is usually somewhere greater than three months but less than one year. A man who has just celebrated his hundredth birthday does not plan his hundred-and-fifth until he is well past 104. Basic common sense.

This just about brings you up to date on where I am at. I have enough horrible illnesses and damage to create an entire case study for a Doctor's Final exam paper. I plod along with my existence of trying to write books, playing with rats and dogs and sorting out the washing. I feel I need to sign off with some great words of wisdom. I am not sure I have any. For those of you not paying attention, I'm a brain-damaged idiot with the memory of a goldfish suffering from Alzheimer's.

I am not one of those infuriating people always trying to find the bright side. Yet day-to-day life is OK, if not brilliant. Some days are really quite positive. Just last week I had a thought that it may even be possible for me to get to host my own fiftieth birthday party (in three years' time). Unlikely, but possible.

On a really good day I may not even introduce Lu to somebody as 'my widow'. Although I am not yet taking the long-term approach of introducing Lu as my 'first wife'.

I have just finished my crosswords for the day and am now writing this concluding paragraph. Whilst doing this, I am drinking a cup of green tea and Ozzy the rat is on my shoulder cleaning the inside of my ears – we all have chores to do. Hardly bliss (at least not for Ozzy) but it is an existence, and plenty have worse.

*****

Acknowledgements and Thank Yous

A few words of appreciation…

Medics: You've had to put up with me and my funny ways. For three years now, you have stopped me being dead. Special mention here to Doctor Naomi Fersht and specialist nurse Eileen Andrews who have kept me going. I love you, NHS.

Carl: "I am of sound mind and body and leave you everything in my estate."

No, I'm not and no I don't! Carl, can you edit this book properly and stop leaving yourself legacies? Anyway, you managed to help me re-organise a lot of the black thoughts in my head into something resembling a book. You structured it so that it is not immediately apparent to a reader that the author has brain damage. Thank you.

Soo: With your superb design skills, you have turned my randomly formatted manuscript into something that looks professional. I am proud to have my name on it. Thank you.

Friends and Family: Fabulous support. Thank you for letting me know I am never out of your thoughts. I'm reciprocating the love.

Proof Readers Andy White, Paula Pitts and Victoria Maxwell-Holroyd: Thank you for helping mend the mistakes caused by brain damage and spellcheck.

Lu: Thank you for sticking with me throughout all of these ordeals. Any sensible wife would have traded me in for an upgrade, but you didn't. Your loyalty and support are awesome. I would not have got this far without you.

23702727R00098

Made in the USA
San Bernardino, CA
29 January 2019